ArtScroll Mesorah Series®

Expositions on Jewish liturgy and thought

Rabbis Nosson Scherman / Meir Zlotowitz
General Editors

Bircas kohanim

THE PRIESTLY BLESSINGS / BACKGROUND, TRANSLATION, AND COMMENTARY ANTHOLOGIZED FROM TALMUDIC, MIDRASHIC, AND RABBINIC SOURCES.

Published by

Mesorah Publications, ltd

Translated and compiled by
Rabbi Avie Gold

An Overview /
Perspective on Peace and Love
by Rabbi Nosson Scherman

FIRST EDITION
First Impression . . . July 1981
Second Impression . . . April 1991

Published by
MESORAH PUBLICATIONS, Ltd.
Brooklyn, New York 11232

Distributed in Israel by
MESORAH MAFITZIM / J. GROSSMAN
Rechov Harav Uziel 117
Jerusalem, Israel

Distributed in Australia & New Zealand by
GOLD'S BOOK & GIFT CO.
36 William Street
Balaclava 3183, Vic., Australia

Distributed in Europe by
J. LEHMANN HEBREW BOOKSELLERS
20 Cambridge Terrace
Gateshead, Tyne and Wear
England NE8 1RP

Distributed in South Africa by
KOLLEL BOOKSHOP
22 Muller Street
Yeoville 2198
Johannesburg, South Africa

THE ARTSCROLL MESORAH SERIES ®
BIRCAS KOHANIM / THE PRIESTLY BLESSINGS
© Copyright 1981 by MESORAH PUBLICATIONS, Ltd.
4401 Second Avenue / Brooklyn, N.Y. 11232 / (718) 921-9000

ISBN:
0-89906-183-4 (hard cover)
0-89906-184-2 (paperback)

Typography by CompuScribe at ArtScroll Studios, Ltd.
4401 Second Avenue / Brooklyn, NY 11232 / (718) 921-9000

Printed in the United States of America by Moriah Offset
Bound by Sefercraft, Inc., Brooklyn, NY

This volume is dedicated to
the memory of

שמואל אליהו בן החבר נפתלי הכהן ז״ל
Fred Samuel Kahn

כ״א ניסן תרע״א — כ״ט כסלו תש״ל
April 19, 1911 — December 8, 1969

הולך תמים ופועל צדק ודובר אמת בלבבו

A man who studied Torah and was guided by its moral and ethical principles in all aspects of life. His warmth, humility, integrity, and strength of character were reflected in a genuine concern for others.
His memory continues to inspire all those whom he touched in his lifetime.

תנצבה

Table of Contents

Preface

One of the most vivid childhood memories of synagogue life is Bircas Kohanim. The little boy under his father's tallis, the hush, the Kohanim singing the chant that has survived time and holocaust, the timeless words of the Torah with which the Creator blesses Israel through the mouths of the Kohanim. Many questions filled our minds over the years. Why only Kohanim? Why do we recite prayers for dreams during Bircas Kohanim? Why are their hands outstretched? Why are we forbidden to watch? What do the blessings mean? Why only on festivals? Like all questions about Jewish law and ritual, these are dealt with fully and extensively in the literature of Torah. Indeed, to find the answer not only constitutes the study of Torah, but fills one with wonder at the profundity of its wisdom. I offer prayers of thanksgiving, therefore, to the Creator for affording me the privilege of writing this volume, thereby not only gaining but also sharing a new appreciation of the mitzvah of Bircas Kohanim.

Many people contributed significantly to the success of this volume; I take this opportunity to express my deep gratitude to them.

RABBI NOSSON SCHERMAN wrote the beautiful Overview, and edited and enriched the entire manuscript. RABBI MEIR ZLOTOWITZ, has encouraged this project from its inception; he read the entire manuscript and offered important suggestions that greatly enhanced the finished work.

REB SHEAH BRANDER has created another example of graphic excellence, especially in overcoming special problems in layouts of the commentary. Perhaps the greatest tribute to his skill is that the ArtScroll Series is so admired for graphic clarity by graphic artists. Additionally, he and Mesorah's other resident Kohen, MR. STEPHEN BLITZ, were very helpful in pointing out matters of special interest to Kohanim and in explaining certain family customs. MRS. SHIRLEY KIFFEL, MRS. SHEVI ASIA, and MISS EDEL STREICHER typeset and continually revised the galleys from manuscript through revisions until the final product. MISS CHANEE FREIER kept the office functioning smoothly throughout. MRS. FAIGIE WEINBAUM read the galleys and page proofs, often under pressure, but always cheerfully and diligently.

Since moving recently to the Kensington neighborhood of Brooklyn, I was privileged to make the acquaintance of HAGAON HARAV AVRAHAM YAAKOV HAKOHEN PAM, שליט"א, Rosh HaYeshivah of Mesivta Torah Vodaath, who has graciously and patiently reviewed and elucidated many of the halachos of Bircas Kohanim. I am grateful to HAGAON HARAV SHIMON SCHWAB שליט"א, rav of the distinguished Khal Adas Yeshurun, for acquainting me with the customs of Frankfurt am Main, which are described frequently in this book. These customs were transplanted to America in 1939 when that community relocated in the Washington Heights section of Manhattan under the guidance of HaGaon HaRav Yosef Breuer, זצ"ל.

The more than one hundred works cited in the commentary include many of the classic commentators, both medieval and more recent, of Scripture, Talmud, Midrash, Halachah and the Siddur. One work merits special mention, for it deals exclusively with the Halachah and liturgy of Bircas Kohanim. First published in 1928, Ateres Paz is one of a series of books relating to specific mitzvos written by HaRav Pinchas Zelig HaKohen Schwartz, זצ"ל הי"ד, of Kleinwardein, Rumania, who was martyred in Auschwitz in 1944.

Everyone at Mesorah Publications is deeply grateful to those who initiated this project — the family of the late FRED SAMUEL KAHN — שמואל אליהו בן החבר נפתלי הכהן ז"ל. It is in his memory that this volume is dedicated. As a Kohen who never took for granted the privilege of blessing Israel, Mr. Kahn often spoke of the need for a volume devoted to Bircas Kohanim. Thanks to his wife, Miriam, their children David and Deborah, Richard and Rhonda, and other members of the family and friends his dream is now fulfilled.

Above all, my sincerest appreciation goes to my wife NECHIE, שתחיה, who has from the very outset established an atmosphere conducive to Torah study in our home, while simultaneously organizing and coordinating her many chessed projects on both the local and national levels. פִּיהָ פָּתְחָה בְחָכְמָה וְתוֹרַת חֶסֶד עַל לְשׁוֹנָה.

יהי רצון מלפניך שתצליחני בדרכי ותן בלבי בינה להבין ולהשכיל ולקים את כל דברי תלמוד תורתך ... ותאריך ימי וימי אשתי ובני ובנותי וימי אמי בטוב ובנעימות ברוב עז ושלום אמן סלה.

אברהם יצחק גאלד
ו' תמוז תשמ"א
6 Tammuz 5741

*An Overview
Perspective on Peace and Love*

◄§ An Overview —
Perspective on Peace and Love

הִלֵּל אוֹמֵר הֱוֵי מִתַּלְמִידָיו שֶׁל אַהֲרֹן הַכֹּהֵן, אוֹהֵב
שָׁלוֹם וְרוֹדֵף שָׁלוֹם אוֹהֵב אֶת הַבְּרִיוֹת וּמְקָרְבָן
לַתּוֹרָה

Hillel says: Be among the disciples of Aaron the Kohen, who was a lover of peace and a pursuer of peace, who was a lover of people and drew them close to the Torah (Avos 1:12).

אָמַר ר׳ אֶלְעָזָר אָמַר ר׳ חֲנִינָא, לֹא נִתְכַּהֵן פִּנְחָס
עַד שֶׁהֲרָגוֹ לְזִמְרִי ... רַב אַשִׁי אָמַר עַד שֶׁשָּׂם
שָׁלוֹם בֵּין הַשְּׁבָטִים

R' Eleazar said in the name of R' Chanina: Phineas did not become a Kohen until he killed Zimri ... Rav Ashi said: [not] until he made peace among the tribes (Zevachim 101b).

I. Aaron the First Kohen

God wishes to bless his people.

Through whom shall the blessing come? Who is worthy enough to inspire in Israel the realization that it must lift itself to meet, to receive, to deserve, God's blessing? And which human vessel is exalted enough to be the medium through which His blessing can be poured upon *'His people Israel with love'*?

The descendants of Aaron and bearers of his holiness are the appropriate ones to convey the blessing of God to the people of God. The *Kohanim* [priests] — descendants of Aaron and bearers of his holiness, the family that earned and accepted the obligation to dedicate their lives to His Temple and His service — *they* are the appropriate ones, the *only* ones who are fit to convey the blessing of God to the people of God.

Knowing that God wishes us always to be blessed and that He chose His *Kohanim* to utter His pronouncement, it is for us to make ourselves worthy of His goodness and to ask His chosen servants to speak the words He assigned them for our benefit *(Sefer HaChinuch)*.

What was it about Aaron and his family that made God vest in them the privilege of being the conduit through which His blessing flows upon Israel?

The question remains, however, what it was about Aaron and his family that made God vest in them the privilege of being the conduit through which His blessing flows upon Israel. True, as *Sefer HaChinuch* says, they are the ones who devoted themselves to His service, but even that is something they were chosen to do. If we can understand by what merit they earned that distinction we can better know the criteria by which all Jews can raise themselves to the level of being blessed and conveying blessing.

Like Spokes

In all history, only two people earned selection to the Kehunah [priesthood] by their own meirts.

In all history, only two people earned selection to the *Kehunah* [priesthood] by their own merits: Aaron — whose four sons were included with him — and Phineas. It stands to reason, therefore, that by understanding the characteristics of these two great Scriptural figures we can understand the essence of the *Kehunah* and the reason why this particular family was chosen to bless Israel.

Indeed, the blessing recited by the *Kohanim* [priests] prior to *Bircas Kohanim* [the Priestly Blessing] contains two unique phrases that set it apart. Whereas other blessings recited before the performance of commandments have the phrase אֲשֶׁר קִדְּשָׁנוּ בְּמִצְוֹתָיו, [God] *Who sanctified us with His commandments*, in *Bircas Kohanim* it is replaced with אֲשֶׁר קִדְּשָׁנוּ בִּקְדֻשָּׁתוֹ שֶׁל אַהֲרֹן, [God] *Who sanctified us with the holiness of Aaron*. Clearly, 'the holiness of Aaron' is the key factor in the choice of his descendants as the agents to confer God's blessing upon Israel. There is another distinctive phrase: the blessing concludes by saying that the *Kohanim* have been commanded לְבָרֵךְ אֶת עַמּוֹ יִשְׂרָאֵל בְּאַהֲבָה, *to bless His people Israel with love*. In the formula of other blessings we never say that the commandment must be performed with love, awe, zeal, or concentration, even though proper intent is essential to the performance of the commandment. Only in the case of *Bircas Kohanim* does the blessing mention a factor other than the physical performance of the commandment — בְּאַהֲבָה, *with love*. It would seem that love is as much a part of *Bircas Kohanim* as the text of the blessing, the upraised hands and spread fingers, and the other Scripturally derived prerequisites described later in this volume.

So two people, Aaron and Phineas, are the quintessential *Kohanim*. And two qualities, Aaron's holiness and love of Israel, are at the root of the Priestly Blessings. Let us try to discover why.

So two people, Aaron and Phineas, are the quintessential Kohanim. And two qualities, Aaron's holiness and love of Israel, are at the root of the Priestly Blessings.

Symbol of Unity

The *Kohen Gadol* had the function of unifying Israel, of helping it become *one* nation. There was a point very early in Jewish history when this concept was challenged. Korach, one of the nation's most distinguished citizens, amassed a significant following and they sought to repudiate the designation of Aaron as the sole *Kohen Gadol*. Since every Jew had heard God's voice at Sinai, they argued, *all* the people are holy — why should only Aaron be declared *Kohen Gadol* (see *Numbers* ch. 16)? Had Korach's rebels had their way, anyone could have declared himself a high priest. Logic appeared to be with him, for it was true, as he claimed, that all Jews are holy and that God resides within them, as individuals and as a nation.

Had Korach's rebels had their way, anyone could have declared himself a high priest. Logic appeared to be with him.

Moses replied, 'Among idolators, there are many religions, and many priests, and they can all congregate in a single house. But as for us — we have but one God, one Ark, one Torah, one altar, and one *Kohen Gadol ...'* (*Bamidbar Rabbah* 18:8; *Tanchuma Korach* 1, 2; see *Rashi* to *Numbers* 16:6).

As for us — we have but one God, one Ark, one Torah, one altar, and one Kohen Gadol.

The point is not that Judaism is monolithic. Each of the Patriarchs developed his own path to the service of God [see Overview to *Lech Lecha*, ArtScroll *Bereishis* vol. II] and each of the twelve tribes had its own uniqueness as demonstrated by Jacob's blessings (*Genesis* 49) and by the history of the tribes. For example, Issachar emphasized Torah study while Zebulun excelled in commerce. Judah governed the nation, Simeon taught it, and Levi served God. In more recent centuries, we have seen such movements within traditional Judaism as Hassidism, Lithuanian scholarship, *Mussar*, Hirschian *Torah-im-Derech Eretz*, and Sephardic mysticism. Nevertheless each of these philosophies and movements have subscribed to the authority of Torah law; none has dared — or even been tempted — to tamper with it.

Like the spokes of a wheel, all tribes and philosophies within Judaism had to be unified by the central authority of Torah Law. As the symbol of Israel's unity, Aaron was part of the people. He wanted them to be free of strife and to be concerned with one another's welfare. The supreme authority of religious law would hardly be sufficient if the nation were torn by strife, jealousy, and discontent. Aaron strove to institute peace among Israel, the peace that exists when man is at harmony with himself because he is living according to the tenets of God for which he was created, and when he is at harmony with his fellows, because he is happy at their good fortune and they assist him in achieving his. By pursuing peace, Aaron unified Israel.

He saw unity as a means, not an end, however. The Mishnah (*Avos* 1:12) describes Aaron as a lover and pursuer of peace and a lover of people, but it does not stop there — the Mishnah concludes by making clear the underlying motive of his activities: וּמְקָרְבָן לַתּוֹרָה, *and he drew* [the people] *close to the Torah*. Aaron recognized that unity can be terribly destructive if turned in the wrong direction, so he taught that only the Torah can be the arbiter of Israel's unity. By his personal example as well as by his preaching, he established the principle that man's noblest goal is to serve God as He commanded and that man's most satisfying success is to take a step toward that goal.

'Good works and a kind heart' are not uncommon among people, but their significance pales unless they are guided by an inner consistency. People have

gone to war over their different definitions —
passionately held beliefs! — of what constitutes
goodness. And kind, but misdirected, hearts have
often nurtured the selfish and hedonistic urges of
man, sapping his ambition to strive for an excellence
that requires him to control the animal in himself.
Because Aaron loved his people *more*, not less, the
peace he fostered was directed toward the purpose of
recognizing one God, one Torah, one altar, and one
law. Had he simply tried to please people without an
underlying philosophy, the result would have been
strife, not only in the nation but within the
individual, as the many fiefdoms of passion and
appetite struggled for control of each human being.

Had he simply tried to please people without an underlying philosophy, the result would have been strife, as the many fiefdoms of passion and appetite struggled for control of each human being.

This strength of commitment infused everything
Aaron did, in the Temple, the street, the home. It
gave direction to his inspirational acts of kindness
and expressions of tact, which the Sages related at
such length:

☐ Aaron would become the good friend of sinners.
Seeing how Aaron sought his company, a sinner
would think, 'Surely I must change my behavior to
be worthy of such a great man's friendship.'

☐ Learning that Reuben and Simeon were engaged
in a bitter dispute, Aaron would accost Reuben and
say, 'You should know that Simeon is heartbroken
over losing your friendship, but he is ashamed to
apologize directly.' Then he would accost Simeon
and tell him the same thing about Reuben. The next
time the two 'enemies' met, they would rush to
embrace one another.

☐ Hearing that an irate husband was baiting his
distraught wife by insisting that she would receive
no further benefits from him unless she spat in
Aaron's eye, Aaron told the poor woman that he had
an eye illness that required the application of saliva.
Would she be kind enough to spit in his eye? She
would thereby satisfy her husband's foolish demand,
and Aaron would demonstrate that a human being's
anguish is more important than the preservation of
his personal dignity.

Aaron would demonstrate that a human being's anguish is more important than the preservation of his personal dignity.

Such deeds put the *Kohen Gadol's* Temple service

in a new perspective. He was not a functionary performing rituals. He was the person entrusted with the primary responsibility for seeking God's forgiveness for the sins and indiscretions of Israel. Aaron — who truly loved Israel and sought its greatest happiness and fulfillment — was the logical person to do this, was he not? The man who prodded sinners to repent, who cajoled disputants to make up, who brought an end to domestic highhandedness — was the same *Kohen Gadol* who atoned for sin and demonstrated that domestic and national unity should be directed toward a way of life that would inspire God Himself to declare 'Who is like My people, Israel, a unique nation on earth!' *(Maharal, Derech Chaim* 1:12).

Priest and People In a profoundly illuminating comment, *Harav Gedaliah Schorr*, זצ״ל, refers to the Talmud's explanation of why there are two different forms of the letter *mem*, מ פְּתוּחָה, the *open* [regular] *mem* and ם סְתוּמָה, the *closed* [final] *mem*, that appears at the end of a word. The Talmud says that they symbolize מַאֲמָר פָּתוּחַ מַאֲמָר סָתוּם, an *open statement* [and] a *closed statement. Rashi* comments that an 'open' statement is a teaching that was meant to be taught and fully explained to the masses while a 'closed' statement is one that is too mystical and esoteric to be understood by any but the greatest, holiest scholars *(Shabbos* 104a).

Harav Schorr cites another explanation. *Every* statement of the Torah has obvious as well as hidden manifestations. We know how a shofar looks and sounds and the prescribed order of its blasts on Rosh Hashanah; that is the *open* revealed manifestation of a shofar, but there is a hidden manifestation as well. The performance of this *mitzvah*, like that of every other, has a distinct function in God's plan for the universe. We do not know how the blowing of a shofar, the affixing of a *mezuzah*, and the eating of matzah effect the universe, but they do. There is a second facet of this *hidden statement* that is implicit in every *mitzvah*. God does not make impossible

We do not know how the blowing of a shofar, the affixing of a mezuzah, and the eating of matzah effect the universe, but they do.

demands. That a *mitzvah* has been made the responsibility of a nation or individual implies that it or he has the inner resources to accomplish whatever the *mitzvah* implies. For example, Israel has the spiritual capacity to sanctify God's Name; therefore, this inner nobility is fleshed out with the tangible requirements of the *mitzvah:* to act in a manner that will bring credit upon God's people, to refrain from any deed that will bring discredit upon the Name, and even to submit to death rather than to cause a desecration of the Name, when the Halachah requires it.

One who loves seeks only the best for the object of his affection. So he teaches the way of Torah, he makes peace among friends and within families, he tries to gain atonement for sins, he unifies his people, and thereby he makes them worthy of the blessing that he so willingly, anxiously, bestows upon them.

If the Kohanim *are commanded to show concern for Israel's well-being by blessing the nation, then we can be sure the descendants of Aaron have the essence of Aaron.* If the *Kohanim* are commanded to show concern for Israel's well-being by blessing the nation, then we can be sure the descendants of Aaron have the inner capacity eternally to continue the loving concern lavished on Israel by their ancestor. Love of Israel was the essence of Aaron.

Shechinah and Nation

בְּשַׁעְתָּא דְּכַהֲנָא רַבָּא הֲוָה לָבִיש בְּחוּשְׁנָא וַאֲפוּדָא שַׁרְיָא עֲלֵיה שְׁכִינְתָּא

At the time when the Kohen Gadol was dressed in the Choshen [breastplate] and Ephod [an apron-like garment], the Divine Presence rested on him (Zohar).

The *Kohen Gadol* was required to wear *eight* special vestments during his service, and the absence of *any* garment invalidated his service, yet the *Zohar makes the presence of the Shechinah dependent upon only the Choshen and Ephod.* The reason may well be the one feature shared exclusively by those two vestments. Upon each, and upon no other, the names of all twelve tribes appeared. Imbedded in the *Choshen* were twelve precious and semi-precious stones upon each of which was engraved the name of one tribe, and set into the shoulder straps of the

Ephod were two such stones, each of them having six names engraved upon it.

The *Kohen Gadol* was not a private person. His role as representative of the nation was symbolized by these two vestments, each of them bearing the names of Israel's tribes, that were indispensable to the service. Whatever he did was the collective deed of the unified nation, and that is what brought the *Shechinah* upon him; he had the additional virtue of Israel's collective presence wherever he went. Thus, the holiness of the *Kohen Gadol* and the holiness of Israel reinforce one another. Aaron — and his successors and descendants — seeks to bring Israel together and his inner affection is expressed in the Torah's command that he bless the nation. In turn, Israel's collective holiness brings the *Shechinah* to the *Kohen Gadol* when the Temple stands, and surely aids the spiritual growth of every *Kohen* nowadays when the only remaining vestige of the Temple service is *Kohen's Bircas Kohanim*.

The holiness of the Kohen Gadol and the holiness of Israel reinforce one another.

II. Kohen by Merit

Defeating Balaam

At first glance, Phineas would seem to be as unlike Aaron as anyone can be. Rather than exercising Aaron's brand of peaceful diplomacy and loving reconciliation, Phineas served the nation by placing himself in danger and aggressively excising sinners from Israel's midst. It happened after the failure of Balaam's attempt to curse Israel. The evil prophet advised his Midianite patrons that they could defeat Israel only by enticing it to immorality, the sin most destructive of Israel's holiness. By the thousands, the young women of Midian descended upon the camp of Israel and succeeded in seducing large numbers of people. Balaam was right. God despises immorality, and a plague began, decimating thousands of Jews. A distinguished Jew, Zimri, leader of a branch of the tribe of Simeon, brazenly and publicly sinned with a Midianite princess named Kazbi. Before such impudent defiance, Moses and the elders were

Stubborn wantonness has an unbridled power. Once unleashed, it defies authority and logic. helpless. Stubborn wantonness has an unbridled power. Once unleashed, it defies authority and logic. Anything Moses said would have caused a backlash. Phineas saw the helplessness of his mentors and the downward plunge of his people.

And he acted.

Phineas killed Zimri and Kazbi with one thrust. The revelers were shocked into a realization of the enormity of their sin, and the plague ended. Phineas had saved the nation (*Numbers* ch. 25 with standard commentaries. See also *Michtav MeEliyahu*).

Surprisingly, Phineas was not a *Kohen*, even though his father was Elazar, Aaron's son and successor when the first *Kohanim* were anointed, it was specified that the honor go to Aaron and his four sons. Their future children would be *Kohanim* automatically, because they would have been born to *Kohanim*. Phineas, however was already living; since he was not designated to become a *Kohen*, he remained a Levite, as he was at birth (*Zevachim* 101b; *Rashi* and *Gur Aryeh* to *Numbers* 25:13).

In reward for his brave act, Phineas was named a *Kohen ... behold, I [God] give him My covenant of peace. To him and his offspring after him shall be the covenant of eternal priesthood in return for his having acted zealously in behalf of his God and having achieved atonement for the Children of Israel* (*Numbers* 25:12, 13, see *Rashi*. See also *Zevachim* 101b).

True Peace

Two questions stand out: why was priesthood the proper reward for his deed, and why was he given the 'covenant of *peace*' for a deed that was by its very nature an aggressive act of war? That Phineas was deserving of reward is beyond question, but it hardly seems right that the twin mantles of Aaron — *Kehunah* and peace — are appropriate to his act.

Harav Schorr explains the uniqueness in Israel of the *Kohen*. He is the one who serves God in a manner permitted no one else. — only a *Kohen* can perform the Temple service. The Israelite sanctifies offerings, the Levite assists in maintaining the Temple, but the

The Kohen serves God in a manner permitted no one else — only a Kohen can perform the Temple service.

essential acts of the service are performed by a *Kohen.* Consequently, he represents the highest levels of aligning human performance with Divine dictates. Phineas, too, did what no one else could. Even Moses was powerless to stop the spiritual insurrection. *No one* could stop Zimri and his followers. The great majority of Jews longed for a way to end the senseless immorality, but only Phineas could do it. He richly earned a reward — and his reward was to be promoted to the only family that was authorized to do what could be done by no one else.

There was another, vital aspect of his act. In their elite position, *Kohanim* do not act on their own behalf. They are representatives of the people even to the point where their vestments are paid for by communal funds, in order to demonstrate, as *R' Hirsch* comments, that they act for all Israel. The Torah testifies that Phineas' zeal was done בְּתוֹכָם, *among* [the people]. He acted not out of contempt for the 'sinful masses,' but because he identified with the suffering of Israel and wanted to rescue his people. If his rashness were to cost him his life, so be it. His life belonged to Israel (*Sfas Emes*).

But peace? Yes, peace. For the mere absence of war can still be a far cry from peace; modern history testifies eloquently to that sad fact. The word שָׁלוֹם is closely related to שָׁלֵם, *complete, wholesome. True* peace is the presence of harmony, when every man fulfills his proper function and every resource is utilized properly. It also means that Israel is protected from outside forces that seek to do it harm. So it was that when Aaron was alive, Israel was protected from attack by עַנְנֵי הַכָּבוֹד, *cloud-pillars* of [God's] *glory.* When Aaron died, the protective clouds departed and Israel was attacked (*Rashi* to *Numbers* 21:1). To permit freedom of action to the Zimris of Israel in the name of 'peace' is an abuse of the word and a danger to the people. Aaron chose to eradicate strife and sin by elevating the combatants and refining the sinners. That path is the best, but sometimes it is inadequate, as in the situation Phineas

A frightful situation in which the only way to exercise love and create peace was to remove the source of strife. faced, a frightful situation in which the only way to exercise love and create peace was to remove the source of strife. True, there were many who condemned Phineas, who insisted that his 'bloody' hands could never be raised in blessing over Israel (see *Rashi, Numbers* 25:11; *Sanhedrin* 82a) but God testified that the truth was otherwise. *Phineas,* not Zimri, represented peace; and *Phineas,* not his detractors, defined the proper role of a *Kohen (Sfas Emes).*

According to Rav Ashi (*Zevachim* 101b), Phineas was not fully accepted as a *Kohen* until many years later when he brought a peaceful conclusion to a situation that could have exploded into a civil war (*Joshua* 22:30-34). Clearly, the blessing of peace remained the essence of the priesthood. Though the common people found it difficult to associate this blessing with the Phineas who killed Zimri, he was vindicated later. Then the man who brought peace to the tribes was recognized as the one who earned the *covenant of peace* by an act that seemed an act of war to the unknowing.

The Kohen Blesses

The climactic blessing of *Bircas Kohanim* is וְיָשֵׂם לְךָ שָׁלוֹם, *may* [God] *grant you peace.* As the Sages teach, peace is the only vessel that can contain Israel's blessing (*Uktzin* 3:12; see *Comm.*). Man can envision infinite dreams and blessings, but all can dissipate unless they are enveloped and protected by the consummate gift of peace. With it, life has meaning and can be guided to fulfillment; without it, the finest gifts can become useless shards.

Man can envision infinite dreams and blessings, but all can dissipate unless they are enveloped and protected by the consummate gift of peace.

Aaron's holiness was best expressed in his enduring image as the man who loved peace, pursued it, and brought it into the everyday lives of his fellow Jews. Because he embodied this ultimate blessing, he was the worthiest to confer blessings upon his people — particularly *Bircas Kohanim,* which is climaxed with the blessing of peace.

A *Kohen* can pronounce the words of *Bircas Kohanim,* but they will be empty unless they are uttered with the sincerity and sanctity of Aaron —

and with the love of Aaron. Therefore the *Zohar* teaches that a *Kohen* who does not love his congregation should not ascend the platform to utter the blessings. Consequently, the *Kohanim* speak of this love and of the unique sort of holiness they inherited from Aaron. This makes them capable of blessing, and with this declaration they proclaim their readiness to walk in the footsteps of the first *Kohen Gadol*.

From Aaron we learn to love peace and to pursue it by bringing love into our midst. From Phineas we learn to love peace and to pursue it by excising evil from our midst.

From Aaron we learn to love peace and to pursue it by bringing love into our midst. From Phineas we learn to love peace and to pursue it by excising evil from our midst. From both we learn the eternal nature of priesthood and peace, and we gain the inspiration to use the teachings of the first to become worthy of the second.

*This Overview is dedicated to
the memory of my uncle,*
הרב הגאון אליהו הכהן מונק זצ״ל
Rabbi Elie Munk זצ״ל
June 5, 1981 / ג׳ סיון תשמ״א

If any Kohen of our generation was the Aaron of his time, it was he. He loved and pursued peace, he loved people and drew them lovingly to Torah. In Ansbach and Paris, his combination of Torah scholarship, total faith in God, utter devotion to community, eloquent tongue, and gifted pen created inspiring and unforgettable chapters of accomplishment. His World of Prayer and Call of the Torah became classics in his lifetime.

יהי זכרו ברוך

Rabbi Nosson Scherman

וַיְדַבֵּר יהוה אֶל־מֹשֶׁה לֵּאמֹר:

And HASHEM spoke to Moses saying,

דַּבֵּר אֶל־אַהֲרֹן וְאֶל־בָּנָיו לֵאמֹר

Speak to Aaron and his sons saying,

כֹּה תְבָרְכוּ אֶת־בְּנֵי יִשְׂרָאֵל

So shall you bless the children of Israel

אָמוֹר לָהֶם:

saying to them:

יְבָרֶכְךָ יהוה וְיִשְׁמְרֶךָ:

May HASHEM bless you and protect you.

יָאֵר יהוה פָּנָיו אֵלֶיךָ וִיחֻנֶּךָּ:

May HASHEM shine His face upon you and be gracious to you.

יִשָּׂא יהוה פָּנָיו אֵלֶיךָ

May HASHEM lift His face to you

וְיָשֵׂם לְךָ שָׁלוֹם:

and may He grant you peace.

וְשָׂמוּ אֶת־שְׁמִי עַל־בְּנֵי יִשְׂרָאֵל

Let them place My Name upon the Children of Israel

וַאֲנִי אֲבָרְכֵם:

and I shall bless them
(Numbers 6:22-27).

~§ Bircas Kohanim in History and Halachah

~§ Kohanim — Successors to the Patriarchs

Said the Holy One, Blessed is He, to Abraham, 'From the time I created My world until now I longed to bless My creatures — as it is written: *God blessed them* [Adam and Eve] *(Genesis* 1:28); *God blessed Noah and his sons (Genesis* 9:1) — but from now on, the blessings are transferred to you. Whomever you wish to bless — bless!' This is the meaning of the verse: *And you shall be a blessing (Genesis* 12:2) ...

After Abraham died, the Holy One, Blessed is He, appeared to Isaac and blessed him — as it is written: *And it was after the death of Abraham that God blessed Isaac, his son (Genesis* 25:11); Isaac in turn blessed Jacob *(Genesis* 27:27-29), and Jacob blessed his twelve sons *(Genesis* 49:28).

After that, the Holy One, Blessed is He, said, 'From now on, the blessings are transferred to the *Kohanim.* They shall bless My children — for just as I said to Abraham, *You shall be a blessing (Genesis* 12:2), I now say to you, *So shall you bless the children of Israel ...' (Bamidbar Rabbah* 11:2; and *Tanchuma, Lech Lecha* 4).

The Patriarchs of Israel were endowed with רוּחַ הַקֹּדֶשׁ, *the Holy Spirit,* which enabled them to perceive the spiritual essence of each person, right to the core of his soul. Because they were not deceived by external appearance, they could bless each person according to his unique needs and potential. [This ability of the Patriarchs is indicated by Scripture's description of Jacob's blessings to his children: *He blessed them, each in accordance with his own blessing did he bless them (Genesis* 49:28).] Because they were capable of composing the blessings most appropriate to each occasion, God did not teach them any particular formula. He merely told Abraham, *'And you shall be a blessing' (Genesis* 12:2).

But in later generations the *Kohanim* would not attain the spiritual level of the Patriarchs; they would be unable to recognize the individual needs of each person and consequently would not know upon whom to bestow which blessing. The Holy One, Blessed is He, therefore, composed the threefold blessing. It is all-inclusive, yet addresses each individual and the entire gamut of his personal requirements. For this reason God instructed Moses to teach Aaron and his sons the precise order of *Bircas Kohanim (Tiferes Zion).*

Another Midrash teaches that the *mitzvah* of *Bircas Kohanim,* which begins with the word כֹּה, **So** *shall you bless the children of Israel,* was given in the merit of the three Patriarchs, about each of whom Scripture uses the word כֹּה, **So.** Regarding Abraham it is written, כֹּה, **So** *shall your offspring be (Genesis* 15:5); about Isaac it is said, *I and the lad* [i.e., Isaac] *will go* כֹּה, **So** *far* [i.e., yonder] *(ibid.* 22:5); and of Jacob the Torah states, כֹּה, **so** *shall you say to the House of Jacob (Exodus* 19:3; *Bereishis Rabbah* 43:8).[1]

The very structure of *Bircas Kohanim* alludes to its relationship with Abraham,

---

1. [The relationship between *Bircas Kohanim* and the three Patriarchs alluded to by the word כֹּה is also suggested by the title כֹּהֵן, *Kohen.* The *gematria* of כֹּהֵן, seventy-five, is exactly three times as much as the *gematria* of כֹּה, twenty-five.]

Isaac, and Jacob. For the three verses represent the three Patriarchs[1], while the fifteen words signify the fifteen years during which the lives of the three overlapped[2] (*Chomas Anach* citing *R' Eliezer of Worms*).

◆§ Names of the Blessing

This Priestly Blessing is known by three names:

(a) בִּרְכַּת כֹּהֲנִים [Bircas Kohanim]. This name has two connotations — the blessing bestowed by the *Kohanim* upon Israel, and the blessing received by the *Kohanim* directly from God in reward for fulfilling His commandment to bless Israel. From the verse [*Numbers* 6:23], *So shall you bless the Children of Israel*, it may be inferred that the blessing pronounced by the *Kohanim* is received only by non-*Kohanim*. Are the *Kohanim* also recipients of the blessing? This question is discussed in the Talmud (*Chullin* 49a). R' Yishmael explains that the subsequent verse, *And I shall bless them*, teaches that the *Kohanim* bless Israel and God blesses the *Kohanim*. R' Akiva, on the other hand, understands that this verse also refers to the Israelites. The *Kohanim shall place My Name upon the Children of Israel and I* [in ratification of that blessing] *shall bless them*, i.e., Israel. That God, in turn, blesses the *Kohanim* is derived from *Genesis* (12:3) when God promises Abraham, *'I will bless those who bless you,'* in return for blessing their fellow Jews the *Kohanim*, like anyone else who blesses the offspring of Abraham, are blessed by God [See *commentary* to וַאֲנִי אֲבָרֲכֵם, p. 84].

(b) נְשִׂיאַת כַּפַּיִם [Nesias Kapayim]. Literally, *raising the hands*, this term is an allusion to the position of the *Kohen's* hands while reciting the blessing [see pp. 41-43 for a discussion of this rule]. Since this requirement is derived from the verse [*Leviticus* 9:22], וַיִּשָּׂא אַהֲרֹן אֶת־יָדָיו, *Aaron raised his hands* [*over the people and he blessed them*], the expected name would be נְשִׂיאַת יָדַיִם, *raising the 'hands,'* yet the Talmud calls it נְשִׂיאַת כַּפַּיִם, *raising the 'palms'*. Among the reasons for this nomenclature is one given in *Shefa Tal* (cited in *Ateres Paz*). *Bircas Kohanim* consists of fifteen words. Each of these words corresponds to a different part of the hand — the first fourteen words, to the fourteen finger bones [two in the thumb,

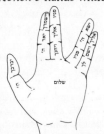

three in each of the other fingers (see diagram)]. The palm represents by the last word, שָׁלוֹם [shalom], *peace*, which is described by the Mishnah (*Uktzin* 3:12) as the only utensil that can contain blessing (see p. 80). The appellation 'raising the palms' alludes to *shalom* without which there can be no blessing.[3]

---

1. [In the list of minimal *kavanos* upon which the *Kohen* must concentrate while bestowing the blessing (p. 48) we find that the first verse is a blessing for offspring — perhaps an allusion to God's words to Abraham, *I shall make of you a great nation* (*Genesis* 12:2), and, *I shall surely bless you and greatly increase your offspring like the stars of the heavens and like the sands of the seashore* (ibid. 22:17).

The blessing of longevity contained in the second verse of *Bircas Kohanim* is symbolized by Isaac whose one hundred and eighty years surpassed Abraham's life span by five years and Jacob's by thirty-three (see *Genesis* 25:7; 35:28; 47:28).

The third blessing, that of שָׁלוֹם, *peace*, refers to Jacob who arrived שָׁלֵם, *in peace*, at the city of Shechem (*Genesis* 33:18, see *Ibn Ezra* there).]

2. Abraham was one hundred years old when Isaac was born (*Genesis* 21:5) and Isaac was sixty years old when Jacob was born (*Genesis* 26:26). Thus Abraham was one hundred sixty years old at Jacob's birth. He died fifteen year later, at the age of 175 (*Genesis* 25:7).

3. *Ben Ish Chai* also maintains that the first fourteen words of *Bircas Kohanim* correspond to the fourteen finger bones of each hand. The final word שָׁלוֹם, *peace*, however — which is the

(c) עֲלִיָּה לַדּוּכָן [Aliyah LaDuchan]. This name means *ascending the platform*. It refers to the location in the *Beis HaMikdash* from where the blessing was bestowed. The *Kohanim* stood on the stairs leading to the Temple proper as they raised their hands to pronounce *Bircas Kohanim* (*Tamid* 7:2). In most synagogues today the *Kohanim* ascend a *duchan*, or platform, in front of the Ark. Although not a necessary condition for *Bircas Kohanim*, use of a *duchan* is preferred. This expression is the source of the term *duchanen* used in the vernacular.

All of the above terms are used interchangeably throughout Rabbinic literature.

◄§ Six Scriptural Requirements

Many of the laws of *Bircas Kohanim* are derived from the stipulation [*Numbers* 6:23] כֹּה תְבָרְכוּ, *so shall you bless*, either by the hermeneutic principle of גְּזֵרָה שָׁוָה [*gezeirah shavah*], *similar phraseology*[1], or by interpreting the word כֹּה, *so*, in its most restrictive sense to mean in *this* manner and only in this manner are you to bless them. This latter view is enunciated by R' Yehudah in the Midrash (*Bamidbar Rabbah* 11:4): 'How may we derive that Moses was told directly by the Holy One, Blessed is He, the precise order in which they [the *Kohanim*] are to bless Israel? — the verse teaches: "*So*" *shall you bless the children of Israel.*'

The Talmud (*Sotah* 38a) and with, minor variations, the Midrash (*Bamidbar Rabbah* 11:4) proceed with the specific requirements governing the mode of the blessings. They must be bestowed:

(a) בִּלְשׁוֹן הַקֹּדֶשׁ, in the Holy Tongue [i.e., Hebrew];
(b) בַּעֲמִידָה, while standing;
(c) בִּנְשִׂיאַת כַּפַּיִם, with raised hands;
(d) בְּשֵׁם הַמְפֹרָשׁ, with the Ineffable Name [this requirement applies only in the *Beis HaMikdash*];
(e) פָּנִים אֶל פָּנִים, face to face; and
(f) בְּקוֹל רָם, in a high voice.

utensil in which the blessing is contained — symbolizes the כּוֹס שֶׁל בְּרָכָה, *cup of blessing*, the cup of wine [held in the palm and grasped by all the fingers] which the Sages have ordained to be used during the performance of many *mitzvos*, such as the wedding ceremony, circumcision, *Kiddush*, and *Havdalah*. This view may also explain the Talmudic dictum, 'Torah Sages increase peace in the world' (*Berachos* 64a). By ordaining the repeated use of the 'cup of blessing' in the performance of *mitzvos*, thereby symbolizing peace, the Sages bring about a constant increase in peace.

Additionally, *Ben Ish Chai* comments, each word of *Bircas Kohanim* supplies the spiritual sustenance of one of the fifteen meals eaten during the week. [The Mishnah (*Peah* 8:7) requires the trustees of the communal charity to supply at least two meals each weekday to the indigent, with a third meal being added on the Sabbath.] Thus, the third Sabbath meal, the concluding meal of the week, corresponds to שָׁלוֹם, *peace*. This correspondence may be used to explain a popular folk custom. When two people meet on a weekday, they say good morning, or evening. On the Sabbath, however, the traditional Hebrew greeting is שַׁבָּת שָׁלוֹם, *Sabbath peace*. This is an allusion to the concluding word of *Bircas Kohanim* which provides the spiritual nourishment of the additional Sabbath meal.

1. [The principle of *gezeirah shavah* involves a comparison of two verses of similar phraseology and the application of what is expressed in one to the other. This principle may be utilized only regarding pairs of words or phrases whose relationship has been transmitted orally from teacher to student all the way back to our master Moses.

Using *Bircas Kohanim* as an example: One of these valid pairs of words is תְבָרְכוּ, *you shall bless*, appearing within the *mitzvah* of *Bircas Kohanim*, and לְבָרֵךְ, *to bless* (*Deuteronomy* 27:12), referring to the *mitzvah* of the recitation of blessings and curses by the Levites when Joshua led the Israelites into Canaan. The relationship between these two words teaches that the conditions necessary to the fulfillment of the Levites' recitation are also applicable to *Bircas Kohanim*. See *Commentary* below for the specific laws derived in this way.]

(a) In the Holy Tongue. To derive the requirement that *Bircas Kohanim* must be pronounced in Hebrew, the principle of *gezeirah shavah* is applied twice. After entering the Land of Canaan, Joshua was to lead the nation to Mount Gerizim and Mount Eival and there conduct the order of blessings and curses ordained by the Torah (see *Deuteronomy* 27:11-26 and *Joshua* 3:33-35). It was mandated that at that time וְעָנוּ הַלְוִיִם ... קוֹל רָם, *the Levites shall respond ... in a high voice (Deuteronomy* 27:14). A similar expression is used to describe God's transmission of the Torah to Moses: *Moses spoke and God* יַעֲנֶנּוּ בְקוֹל, *responded to him in a voice (Exodus* 19:19). Both verses use variations of the words ענה and קוֹל; from this similarity of expression, the Sages expound that just as God spoke to Moses in the Holy Tongue so must the Levites at Mount Gerizim pronounce the blessing in Hebrew *(Sotah* 33a; *Tosafos, ad loc*, s.v., וְעָנִיתָ וְאָמַרְתָּ).

Further comparison yields a second *gezeirah shavah*, by means of which a law of *Bircas Kohanim* is derived from the blessing of the Levites. In the commandment of *Bircas Kohanim*, the *Kohanim* are told, *So shall you bless* [תְּבָרְכוּ] ..., and of the blessings at Mount Gerizim it is stated: *These [tribes] shall stand to bless* [לְבָרֵךְ] *the nation (Deuteronomy* 27:12). The related expressions for 'blessing' are likened to one another to teach that just as the blessings at Mount Gerizim were recited in the Holy Tongue (as established through the above *gezeirah shavah*), so must *Bircas Kohanim* be spoken in Hebrew.

R' Yehudah holds that the requirement of the Holy Tongue is implicit in the verse, even without the use of a *gezeirah shavah*. According to him, the word כֹּה, *in this manner* [and in no other], means *with these exact words shall you bless ... (Sotah* 38a).[1]

(b) While Standing. The same *gezeirah shavah* discussed above — *So shall you bless* (תְּבָרְכוּ) and, *These shall "stand" to bless* (לְבָרֵךְ) — yields the requirement that just as the twelve tribes on the mountainsides stood, so must the *Kohanim* stand while blessing the nation.

------

1. Regarding the supremacy of Hebrew as the language of prayer and blessings *Chasam Sofer* writes: Although one may fulfill his obligation of prayer [i.e., to recite the *Shemoneh Esrei*] in any language, this leniency applies only in unusual circumstances and not to the regular communal prayer services. These must be conducted in the Holy Tongue in which the *Anshei Knesses HaGedolah* [see p. 39 and footnote] wrote the prayers. That this body of Sages chose the language of Hebrew can be attributed neither to the tongue's popularity at the time nor to the nation's fluency in it. Scripture clearly states the contrary: *And their children*, [i.e. of the Jews returning to *Eretz Yisrael* from Babylon] — *half of them spoke the language of Ashdod and were unfamiliar with the Judean tongue, and* [others spoke] *the language of each and every nation* [from which they came] *(Nehemiah* 13:24; see *Rambam, Tefillah* 1:4). If communal prayer were permitted in the vernacular or in any language other than the Holy Tongue, the *Anshei Knesses HaGedolah* would have written the prayers in the language of Ashdod, spoken by the largest segment of Jewry at that time. Obviously then, the use of Hebrew must be ascribed to more than its popularity.

The choice of the Holy Tongue for the prayers and blessings may be explained by analogy with the language used in a king's court. No human monarch conducts his official business in a foreign language — even one in which he is fluent. Ceremonies of state, proclamations to the populace, official documents, all utilize the language of the land [the King's English, so to speak]. How unseemly it would be then to use an alien tongue in the service of the King of Kings. The Holy Tongue is His — in it He addresses His prophets. It is the language in which He wrote the Torah. With it He created the world and named His creatures [אָדָם, *Adam*, means 'from the earth'; חַוָּה, *Chavah* (Eve), means 'mother of all the living'; etc.]. Therefore it is the language in which He may be approached by His subjects, in their prayers, supplications, and blessings.

Additionally, prayers are a temporary — albeit centuries long — substitute for the Temple service. They were instituted in accordance with the verse: *We shall pay* [i.e., substitute] *for the oxen with our lips (Hosea* 14:3). But only the Holy Tongue contains the nuances which

The Tanna R' Nassan disagrees. He derives the requirements of standing from the principle of הֶקֵּישׁ [hekeish], comparison.[1] Scripture speaks of the Temple service of the Kohanim and their pronouncing Bircas Kohanim in the same verse [Deuteronomy 21:5], '... to serve Him [the Temple service] and to bless [Bircas Kohanim] in the Name of HASHEM'. But we are also taught that the Kohanim must perform the Temple service while standing — as the verse [Deuteronomy 18:5] states: ... to stand, to serve in the Name of HASHEM. The juxtaposition of Bircas Kohanim with the Temple service implies the Kohanim must also stand while reciting their blessing (Sifre; Sotah 38a as emended by Rashash in his commentary to Bamidbar Rabbah 11:4).

Most authorities consider the requirement that the Kohen stand erect to be an integral part of the Bircas Kohanim, and not subject to any leniency. This view is summed up in Mishnah Berurah (128:51): 'A Kohen who is weak and cannot stand without support may not raise his hands [to pronounce the blessing]; this posture [i.e., leaning on something for support] is tantamount to sitting.'

Although it is incumbent upon the Kohanim to stand during the blessing, the congregation may sit.[2] This lenient ruling is apparent from Zohar[3] (Magen Avraham 128:22). Nevertheless, the prevalent custom calls for everyone to stand with awe and solemnity before the Kohanim (Mishnah Berurah 128:51).

Shem Chadash (to Sefer Yereim 15) cites the verse the entire assemblage drew near and 'stood' before HASHEM (Leviticus 9:5) as an allusion to this custom.

(c) With Raised Hands. Once again the Talmud employs the principle of gezeirah shavah to derive the requirement that the Kohanim pronounce the blessing with raised hands. The Kohanim are commanded, So shall you bless ... and elsewhere it is written, And Aaron raised his hands toward the nation and he blessed them (Leviticus 9:22) — just as Aaron's blessing was pronounced with raised hands, so must Bircas Kohanim be pronounced with raised hands (Sotah 38a).

Although praying with raised hands is found often in Scripture [e.g., I Kings 8:22; Psalms 63:5], this form of prayer, which has become prevalent among Gen-

---

imbue the words with the kavanos [intentions] and tikkunim [release and elevation of the holiness inherent in every being] effected by the Temple service. Thus it is the only language which may be utilized in the communal prayers (Responsa Chasam Sofer, VI, 84).

1. [The principle of hekeish is based on the juxtaposition of two laws or phrases. Since the Torah places two unrelated subjects next to one another, the implication is that the laws of the two subjects apply to one another. This principle can be used only with relation to subjects set forth to Moses at Sinai.]

2. [Although the tribes on the two mountainsides were required to stand, we do not derive from the gezeirah shavah that the congregation must stand during Bircas Kohanim. The tribes were participants in the blessings, not mere recipients. Every member of the nation had a part in the recitation of the blessings and curses there — the Levites pronounced them as ordained in the Torah while the Israelites responded amen in a high voice. This amen was an integral part of the pronouncements at Mount Gerizim and Mount Eival. In the case of Bircas Kohanim, however, the communal response of amen is not a necessary condition in all instances. The halachah declares that if a synagogue congregation consists of exactly ten Kohanim and no other person is present, all ten Kohanim ascend the duchan, even though no one will respond amen.]

3. [The citation given in Magen Avraham — Zohar, parashas Naso, folio 228 — is no doubt a copyist's error. For one, that page belongs to parashas Pinchas and secondly, it makes no mention of Bircas Kohanim. Perhaps Magen Avraham means folio 147a which reads: 'At the time the Kohen raises his hands, the congregation must "sit" in fear and awe ...']

tiles, has fallen into disfavor among Jews. This rejection of a previously acceptable mode of worship has its basis in the Torah. During the time of the Patriarchs the erection of a מַצֵּבָה [matzeivah], standing stone or pillar [i.e., a single stone erected as an altar, usually used for libations rather than animal sacrifice], was considered a valid means of offering thanksgiving to the Creator. On three separate occasions Scripture records that Jacob set up matzeivos (Genesis 28:18; 31:45 and 35:14). Yet in Deuteronomy (16:22) we are taught: Do not set up a matzeivah for yourself, that which HASHEM, your God, despises. Rashi (ad loc., based on Sifre) explains that although in the time of the Patriarchs the matzeivah was acceptable, it became prohibited when such altars became the standard mode of Canaanite idol worship. [A full discussion of the changing status of the matzeivah appears in ArtScroll Bereishis, p. 1242.] Similarly, praying with upraised hands, although not forbidden, has fallen into disuse in the synagogue service (Hagahos R' Akiva Eiger, Orach Chaim 89, citing Be'er Sheva 74).

Nevertheless, it is only during prayer that the hands are no longer upraised. This position remains a necessary condition of Bircas Kohanim. In fact, the consensus of authorities is: 'One whose hands are so unsteady that he cannot hold them high should not recite Bircas Kohanim, for this posture is required regardless of the circumstances. Even if one were to support his hands with straps attached to his hat, this would not be acceptable, for the Kohen is required to raise his hands by his own power. However, if one is capable of lifting his hands for the short time it takes to pronounce each word of the blessing, then even though he lowers his hands between words, he may recite Bircas Kohanim' (Mishnah Berurah 148:52).

The significance of the Kohanim's raised hands is described by the Midrash: My Beloved is like a deer ... Behold He stands behind our wall, looking through the windows, peering through the lattices. My Beloved replied and said to me ... (Song of Songs 2:9-10). The Midrash explains that these verses refer to Bircas Kohanim.

My Beloved is like a deer — just as a deer leaps from place to place, from fence to fence, from tree to tree ... so does the Holy One, Blessed is He, leap from synagogue to synagogue [at the time of Bircas Kohanim (Maharzu)] in order to bless Israel ...

Behold He stands behind our wall — this passage refers to the synagogues and study halls ... for when the Holy One, Blessed is He, commanded Aaron and his sons, 'So shall you bless...' all of Israel complained. 'Master of the universe, You tell the Kohanim to bless us! We are interested in receiving Your blessings, those that issue directly from Your mouth ...'

The Holy One, Blessed is He, replied, 'Although I have told the Kohanim to bless you, I too, shall stand among them and bless you.'

The Midrash continues that the Kohanim position their hands to symbolize that God stands behind them, as it were, while they bless Israel. Their fingers are spread in a manner that suggests 'windows in the synagogue walls,' through which God looks on as His people are blessed. The exact position of the fingers is discussed on p. 41-42. The Midrashic exegesis is as follows: [He is] looking through the windows [i.e., over the shoulders of the Kohanim and between their heads (Maharzu)] peering through the lattices [i.e., through the spaces between their extended fingers (Maharzu)].

My Beloved replied and said to me — [what did He say? God gave the promise following the text of Bircas Kohanim:] 'And I [Myself] shall bless them' (Bamidbar Rabbah 11:2; Shir HaShirim Rabbah 2:9).

(d) With the Ineffable Name. The phrase 'so shall you bless' implies that [the entire blessing including] the Ineffable Name should be pronounced exactly as it is written. Even if you do not accept the validity of this inference, the verse later states, 'And they shall place שְׁמִי, My Name' — that is to say, the Name which is unique to Me[1] (Sotah 38a).

That the Name as it is written may be pronounced only in the Temple [see "In the Beis HaMikdash," p. 35], but not elsewhere, is derived through a *gezeirah shavah* [see footnote, p. 29]. Our verse states: וְשָׂמוּ אֶת־שְׁמִי, *and they shall place My Name*. Another verse describes the Temple as: *The site which HASHEM, your God, has chosen from among all of your tribes*, לָשׂוּם אֶת־שְׁמוֹ שָׁם, *to place His Name there* (Deuteronomy 12:5). Just as *to place His Name* refers only to the Temple, so, too, *they shall place My Name* [meaning the proper pronunciation] refers to that chosen spot.

R' Yoshiah offers an alternative derivation: *Every place where I would have My Name mentioned, I shall come to you and bless you* (Exodus 20:21). Can the verse mean literally *everywhere*? [— i.e., we have been taught that God's Name is not to be mentioned (Rashi; see footnote).] The verse must be interpreted as if the word order were reversed: '*Every place where I come to you to bless you* [i.e., where the *Shechinah* is present — the Tabernacle in the wilderness and Shiloh, and later in the Temple in Jerusalem (Rashi)] *there I would have My Name mentioned* — i.e., pronounced' (Sotah 38a; see also *Bamidbar Rabbah* 11:4).

(e) Face to Face. The Talmud cites a *baraisa*: The Torah's expression, *So shall you bless ...* implies that the blessing should be bestowed 'face to face', i.e., while the *Kohanim* and the nation are facing each other, since the normal manner for someone pronouncing a blessing is to stand face to face with the recipient. Even if you reject this inference, the verse continues: *Say to them ...* — which means as a person speaks with his fellow [i.e., face to face] (Sotah 38a).

In codifying the laws of *Bircas Kohanim*, Rambam (Hil. Tefillah 14:11) enumerates all six requirements derived by the Talmud. *Shulchan Aruch (Orach Chaim* 128:14), however, offers an abridged listing: '... in the Holy Tongue, while standing, with raised hands, and in a loud voice,' but omits 'with the Ineffable Name' and 'face to face'.

[The omission of 'with the Ineffable Name' is readily understandable, for in *Rambam's* words 'this requirement only applies in the Temple'. *Shulchan Aruch* codifies only laws that are applicable at present, unlike *Rambam* (who includes הִלְכְתָא לִמְשִׁיחָא, *laws pertaining to Messianic times*, when services will once again be performed in the rebuilt Temple) but *Shulchan Aruch's* omission of 'face to face' presents a problem.]

One solution is that although this requirement is not listed in 128:14 together with the others, nevertheless, *Shulchan Aruch* has mentioned it earlier (128:11), albeit in passing: 'As they turn *their faces toward the congregation*, they recite the prior blessing, "... Who has sanctified us with the holiness of Aaron..." '. And later *Shulchan Aruch* (128:23) states: 'While the *Kohanim* bless the congregation, the

---

1. The interpretation of the term שְׁמִי, *My Name*, as a reference to the Ineffable Name being pronounced as it is written is presumably based on the Talmud's explanation of another verse:

Moses asked of God: *When I come to the Children of Israel and say to them, 'The God of your ancestors has sent me to you,' and they will respond, 'What is His Name?' What shall I say to them?*

God replied: י־ה־ו־ה, *HASHEM, God of Your ancestors*, זֶה שְׁמִי, *this is My Name eternally*, וְזֶה זִכְרִי, *and this is My Mention in every generation* (Exodus 3:13,15).

[The Talmud finds this last passage difficult, for although the verse records only one name — the Ineffable Four Letter Name — it repeats the demonstrative pronoun זֶה, *this*, the repetition indicating that two Names are under discussion.]

R' Avina explains the passage: The Holy One, Blessed is He, meant, 'Not as My Name is written, is it pronounced [or mentioned].' *This is My Name* alludes to the way we spell God's Name, י־ה־ו־ה; *this is My Mention* refers to our pronunciation of the Name, as if it were spelled אֲדֹנָי, *Adonai* (Pesachim 50a).

congregation should not look [at them] but should lower their eyes ... yet they should be *face to face* with the *Kohanim.'* Thus the requirement is codified *(Pri Chadash* citing *Knesses HaGedolah).* [According to this view, face to face seems to be a necessary condition, the lack of which would invalidate the performance of *Bircas Kohanim.*]

An opposing opinion is proposed by *R' Shneur Zalman of Liadi (Shulchan Aruch HaRav* 128:23). He maintains that although it is *preferable* [לְכַתְּחִלָה] for the *Kohanim* to face the congregation, the *Bircas Kohanim* is not invalidated if they fail to do so. Consequently, *Shulchan Aruch* omits this law from the list of absolute requirements. He adduces a Talmudic discussion *(Sotah* 38b) to prove his point:

Adda taught in R' Simlai's name that in a synagogue where only *Kohanim* are present, all of them raise their hands for *Bircas Kohanim.*

R' Zeira explained that although no people are present to receive the blessing, the *Kohanim's* words apply to 'their brethren in the fields,' who are unable to cease their labors and come to town for services. [This discussion refers to *Eretz Yisrael* where the *Kohanim* ascend the *duchan* daily.] In reply to the objection raised in the Talmud that those standing behind the *Kohanim* are excluded from the blessing, R' Zeira distinguished between one purposely standing behind the *Kohanim,* even though he could have stood before them, and one who is a victim of extenuating circumstances.

From R' Zeira's teaching, *Shulchan Aruch HaRav* concludes that the 'face to face' requirement is sometimes waived. Thus, although ideally the condition should be met, if it is not, the blessing is nevertheless valid.

(f) In a High Voice. That Bircas Kohanim must be pronounced in a high voice is derived from the words אָמוֹר לָהֶם, *say to them* — i.e., speak to them as one speaks with his fellow [loud enough to be heard clearly, which would mean by all members of the congregation] *(Sotah* 38a).

The rule necessitating a high voice is actually included in the *gezeirah shavah* from which we have previously derived that *Bircas Kohanim* must be spoken in the Holy Tongue [see p. 30] and while standing *[ibid.].* Just as the blessings at Mount Gerizim were pronounced in קוֹל רָם, *a high voice (Deuteronomy* 27:14), so must *Bircas Kohanim.* The Talmud's derivation of this rule from the words *say to them* is necessary only in the view of R' Yehudah who, rejecting the *gezeirah shavah,* reads the requirement to utilize the Holy Tongue directly into the verse, *So shall you bless (Tosafos, Sotah* 38a).

With reference to the blessings at Mount Gerizim, the Talmud *(Yerushalmi Sotah* 7:2) teaches that רָם, *high,* does not mean 'loud' but 'exalted'. Accordingly the Sages there offer two interpretations for קוֹל רָם:

— *'The voice of the Exalted One'* [as in רָם עַל כָּל גּוֹיִם ה', HASHEM *is exalted over all nations (Psalms* 113:4)], i.e., God's voice, which merged with the voices of the Levites at Mount Gerizim as they pronounced their blessings.

— Or קוֹל רָם may be translated *an exalted voice.* The Levites neither shouted their words nor whispered them. Rather they spoke in a voice between these two extremes.

Although *Yerushalmi* refers to the blessings at Mount Gerizim, *Tur (Orach Chaim* 128) cites this passage as referring to *Bircas Kohanim.* This citation is in accord with *Tosafos'* opinion [cited above] that the requirement of a high voice is derived through a *gezeirah shavah* which compares *Bircas Kohanim* to the blessings at Mount Gerizim *(Bach).*

The *Kohanim* should bless the nation in such a manner that the רָם, *Exalted One,* approves of their blessing. In other words, they should pronounce *Bircas Kohanim* with all their heart and with full knowledge that they are performing the entire *mitzvah* precisely as they are required to. Then God will certainly add His voice to theirs *(Perishah* 128:18).

Although the words קוֹל רָם are not taken in the literal sense of *a loud voice*, nevertheless, there are times when the Kohanim *must* shout out their blessing — as in the presence of a very large congregation — for it is mandatory that every person present hear the blessing. It seems obvious, therefore, that one whose voice is so weak that he can speak only in a whisper may not recite *Bircas Kohanim*. He should preferably leave the synagogue before the *chazzan* reaches the blessing of רְצֵה (*Mishnah Berurah* 128:53).

⋖§ In the Beis Hamikdash

The Mishnah (*Tamid* 5:1) describes the order of morning prayers that was followed by the *Kohanim* participating in the daily Temple service. These prayers concluded with עֲבוֹדָה, *Avodah* — a blessing invoking Divine acceptance of their Temple Service [similar to the one (רְצֵה) found in our *Shemoneh Esrei*] — and a second blessing that the Mishnah calls *Bircas Kohanim*.

The identity of this latter blessing is a point of dispute among the commentators. *Rashi* (*Berachos* 11b) identifies it as the name implies and comments that the purpose of *Bircas Kohanim* at this point is לְבָרֵךְ אֶת הָעָם, *to bless the nation*. Thus the *Kohanim* did not merely utter a prayer [see below], but actually raised their hands to bestow the blessings upon the people.

Tosafos questions this view by pointing out a contradiction. In a later mishnah in *Tamid* (7:2) the tanna states that the *Kohanim* raised their hands to bless the nation at the completion of the morning service [the full text of that mishnah is quoted below]. According to *Rashi*, therefore, they would have bestowed the *Bircas Kohanim* twice each morning. However, the Talmud (*Taanis* 26b) clearly limits the blessing to once each morning.

Based on this contradiction, *Tosafos* proposes that at this point in the service *Bircas Kohanim* was recited not as a blessing of the people, with raised hands, but in the manner of the *chazzan* reading it today. *Rosh* (*Tamid* 5:1) adds that they merely prayed for Divine acceptance of the blessing they would bestow upon the nation *later* in the day, when the morning service was completed. They recited the same formula as our *chazzanim*, but omitted the three verses which form the core of the blessing.

According to each of the opinions cited above, the term *Bircas Kohanim* as used in *Tamid* 5:1 refers to the blessings usually called by that name, either in its full form or in an abridged version.

Rambam (*Commentary* to *Tamid* 5:1 and *T'midin U'Mussafin* 6:4), followed by *Ravad*, takes a different view. The words *Bircas Kohanim* of the mishnah refer to the final benediction of the *Shemoneh Esrei* which begins שִׂים שָׁלוֹם, *Sim Shalom*. [According to this opinion, the mishnah calls this blessing *Bircas Kohanim* because the priestly blessings are normally pronounced during the recitation of *Sim Shalom* (*Kessef Mishneh*, *T'midin U'Mussafin* 6:4) and the common theme of both is שָׁלוֹם, *peace* (*Rashash, Tamid* 5:1, based on *Bamidbar Rabbah* 11:7).]

Thus we find three basic interpretations of the *Bircas Kohanim* described by the mishnah as recited during the pause in the morning service:

Rashi — the full blessing was pronounced with raised hands;

Tosafos and *Rosh* — the same formula currently uttered by the *chazzan* during his repetition of *Shemoneh Esrei* was recited by the *Kohanim*, invoking God's acceptance of the blessing to be given later; and

Rambam and *Ravad* — the term is not used in its conventional meaning but refers to *Sim Shalom*.

A later mishnah in *Tamid* (7:2; parts of which also appear in *Sotah* 37b-38a) relates that at the conclusion of the daily morning service all Kohanim present would 'come and stand on the stairs leading to the Temple ... and they would bless the nation with a single blessing, which elsewhere [i.e., in the synagogues] is pronounced as three'. [This refers to a difference in procedure between the synagogue and the Temple. Everywhere but in the Temple, the congregation responds *amen* after each verse of *Bircas Kohanim* thus separating it into three parts. In the Temple, however, *amen* is not said; but after the *Kohanim* finish all three verses the assemblage responds, 'Blessed is the Name, the Glory of His Kingship is forever and ever' *(Sotah* 40b and *Rashi)*]. In the Temple they pronounced the Name as it is written [i.e., the Ineffable Name — יְ־הֹ־וָ־ה]: elsewhere, it is pronounced as if it were spelled אֲדֹנָי, *Adonai,* literally *my Lord;* and elsewhere they raised their hands to shoulder level, while in the Temple they raised their hands above their heads — except for the *Kohen Gadol* who did not raise his hands higher than his צִיץ, *forehead plate* [upon which was engraved the words קֹדֶשׁ לַה', *Holy to HASHEM*] *(Rashi;* see *Exodus* 28:36).

□ **Shimon HaTzaddik — Kohen Gadol.** Up to and including the forty-year tenure of Shimon HaTzaddik *(the Righteous),* successor to Ezra, and the second *Kohen Gadol* of the Second Temple era, the *Kohanim* continued to pronounce the Ineffable Name as it is written (יְ־הֹ־וָ־ה) when blessing the masses in the Temple Courtyard. Utterance of the Name was proper then, for many manifestations of the Divine Presence were evident in the Temple. Among them were: the westernmost flame of the Menorah burned continuously; although only two logs were added to the altar fires each morning, the fires waxed greater throughout the day; miracles occurred with the *Omer,* the Two Loaves and the *Panim* Bread.[1] After Shimon HaTzaddik's passing these manifestations disappeared *(Yoma* 39a; *Tosefta Sotah* 13:8).

The Talmud recounts the last three weeks of his life:

After Yom Kippur of the year in which Shimon HaTzaddik died, he told his fellow *Kohanim* that this would be his last year. When asked how he could be sure, he

1. On the second day of Passover an offering was brought consisting of an *omer* (a measure equal to the volume of water displaced by 43.2 eggs) of crushed barley grains (see *Leviticus* 2:14-16 and 23:9-11). As with other meal offerings, a fistful (קוֹמֶץ) of the flour was separated from the rest and offered upon the altar. The remaining flour was eaten by the *Kohanim* (see *Rambam, T'midin U'Mussafin* 7:12).

On Shavuos two loaves of leavened bread, made of flour from the 'new' crop of wheat (חָדָשׁ), were offered in the Temple *(Leviticus* 23:16-17). No part of this offering was placed upon the altar, since leavened bread may not be placed on the altar *(Leviticus* 2:11).The loaves were 'waved' [תְּנוּפָה], to the four points of the compass, and upward and downward (see *Leviticus* 2:12). In conjunction with the 'two loaves', two sheep were sacrificed as peace offerings (שַׁלְמֵי צִבּוּר) and a he-goat as a sin offering *(Leviticus* 23:17-20). After the sacrifice the two loaves were given to the *Kohanim* to eat (one was given to the *Kohen Gadol* and one to all the other *Kohanim; Rambam, T'midin U'Mussafin* 8:11).

Every Sabbath twelve loaves known as לֶחֶם הַפָּנִים, *the Panim bread,* were arranged on the Golden Table in the Temple, in two tiers of six each. They remained there until the next Sabbath, when they would be replaced with twelve fresh loaves. A spoonful of frankincense [לְבוֹנָה] was placed next to each tier. Upon removal of the loaves, the frankincense would be offered upon the altar and loaves would be distributed among the *Kohanim* who served during the previous and the coming weeks (see *Succah* 5:7-8).

Since virtually all the *Kohanim* were present in the Temple on the pilgrimage festivals, the number of portions to be distributed from the *Omer* and the *Two Loaves* was so great that each *Kohen* could expect only a tiny share, barely a taste. Although the *Panim* Bread consisted of twelve loaves and was usually divided between two of the twenty-four watches of *Kohanim,* on a festival that fell on the Sabbath all *Kohanim* would receive a share. Again only a tiny portion could be expected. During Shimon HaTzaddik's tenure, however, every *Kohen* received a full olive's bulk of each of these offerings. Moreover, the portions were so filling that this small amount satisfied most of the *Kohanim,* while others were able to eat their fill and have some left over. With Shimon HaTzaddik's passing, these miracles ended *(Yoma* 39a; *Tosefta Sotah* 13:8).

replied, "Every Yom Kippur an old man, garbed in white and cloaked in white, would meet me and accompany me into the Holy of Holies and escort me out. This year I was met by an old man garbed in black and cloaked in black. He accompanied me into the Holy of Holies but did not leave with me."[1]

Shimon HaTzaddik became ill after Succos and died seven days later. From that day forward, his fellow *Kohanim* refrained from blessing with the Ineffable Name *(Menachos 109b; Yoma 39b)*.

◄§ Bircas Kohanim on Weekdays, Sabbaths and Festivals

'The *Kohanim* are commanded to bless Israel every day,' writes *Rambam* in his preface to *Hilchos Tefillah*. Nor does the Talmud suggest that there are days on which the *Kohanim* do *not* ascend the *duchan*. Additionally, Halachah requires them to ascend everytime the *chazzan* repeats *Shemoneh Esrei; Shacharis, Mussaf, Minchah, Ne'ilah*. Yet, for many centuries *Bircas Kohanim* has been omitted from the daily and Sabbath services in virtually every community outside of *Eretz Yisrael* and Egypt. In most places, even on festivals the *Kohanim* do not ascend the *duchan* except at *Mussaf*,[1] and nowhere do they ascend during *Minchah*.

The omission of *Bircas Kohanim* during *Minchah* is mentioned in the Talmud *(Taanis 26b)*. There it is explained that since *Minchah* follows the midday meal, the Rabbis decreed that the blessing be omitted lest the *Kohanim* drink alchoholic beverages during the meal, thereby disqualifying themselves from pronouncing the blessing.

□ **In the Diaspora — Only on Festivals.** Regarding the limitation of *Bircas Kohanim* to festivals, *Rama* (128:44) explains that *Bircas Kohanim* may be pronounced only in a joyous atmosphere; hence, on weekdays when people are preoccupied with earning a livelihood — and even on the Sabbath when such mundane thoughts are difficult to avoid — *Bircas Kohanim* may not be pronounced. However, on festivals when the *Mussaf* service precedes the festive meal, a joyous mood *does* prevail; hence, *Bircas Kohanim* may be pronounced.[2]

According to *Rama's* reasoning, it would follow that on joyless days such as public fasts, *Bircas Kohanim* should not be recited, yet the Mishnah *(Taanis 4:1)* clearly states that the *Kohanim* raise their hands on these days. Therefore, other authorities seek additional explanations for its omission from the daily prayers.

Responsa Beis Ephraim theorizes that since very few *Kohanim* have positive documentary proof of their בְּהֻנָּה, *priestly descent*, the recitation of *Bircas Kohanim*, which is a privilege permitted only to qualified priests, is kept to a minimum. However, the early inhabitants of Jerusalem who did not wander in exile as much as those living in the Diaspora generally had such documentation; hence, the custom

---

1. When R' Abuhu related this incident to his students, one of them asked, 'Scripture teaches: No man (אָדָם) shall be in the Sanctuary when he [the Kohen Gadol] comes into the Holy for the atonement service — until he leaves (Leviticus 16:17). And we have been taught that this prohibition includes even the angels of whom it is written: As for the semblances of their faces — the face of a man (אָדָם) ... (Ezekiel 1:10).'

R' Abuhu replied, 'Why do you think it was a man or an angel who accompanied him? I say it was the Holy One, Blessed is He, Himself [manifesting Himself in this guise]' (Yerushalmi Yoma 5:2).

1. A notable exception is the community of Frankfurt am Main where the Kohanim ascend the duchan at both Shacharis and Mussaf on each festival, and, on Yom Kippur, at Ne'ilah as well.

2. On Yom Kippur the Kohanim raise their hands because of the joy inherent in receiving forgiveness and atonement (Mishnah Berurah 128:166).

in Jerusalem and some other cities in *Eretz Yisrael* to pronounce *Bircas Kohanim* every day. Once the custom was adopted, it remained in effect even after conditions changed.

Alternatively, *Sefer Moadim U'Zemanim* notes that in the Temple, *Bircas Kohanim* was pronounced only at the time of עֲבוֹדָה, [*the sacrificial*] *service*, of a קָרְבַּן צִבּוּר, *communal offering (Tosafos, Sotah* 38a). The Sages frequently refer to *Shemoneh Esrei* as עֲבוֹדָה, *service*, for it is intended as a substitute for the *sacrificial service of the Temple*. If a proper quorum listens attentively to the *chazzan's* repetition of *Shemoneh Esrei*, it can be considered equivalent to a *communal* offering.

In Talmudic times, when many people were unable to recíte the prayers correctly, they fulfilled their obligation to pray by listening intently to the *chazzan's* repetition and answering *'amen.'* It was therefore taken as a matter of course that the *chazzan's Shemoneh Esrei* was a communal service at which *Bircas Kohanim* should be recited. Nowadays, when all people pray from *siddurim*, they do not rely on the *chazzan* to fulfill their obligation. Since the congregation is not very attentive to his recitation, it is not considered a communal service, and *Bircas Kohanim* is not pronounced. On festivals, however, since people are not preoccupied with anything but the spirit of the festival, they will listen attentively to the *chazzan* even though they have already fulfilled their individual obligation.

Similarly in Jerusalem, since the early settlers dedicated their lives to the service of God and were not preoccupied with mundane thoughts they adopted the Sephardic custom of pronouncing the blessing every day. Among the Sephardim, in turn, there were many worshipers who were unable to read the prayers, and, therefore, listened attentively to the *chazzan* in order to fulfill their obligation. For this reason these communities kept the Talmudic custom of pronouncing *Bircas Kohanim* every day.

Over the years various *Rabbanim* attempted to reinstitute *Bircas Kohanim* in the Diaspora on a daily basis, but none succeeded. *Chut HaMeshulash* records that *R' Nassan Adler* (teacher of *Chasam Sofer*) would ascend the *duchan* daily in his private synagogue in Frankfort, although this custom was not accepted by the rest of the community.

Netziv recalls having heard from his grandfather that the *Vilna Gaon* once decided to reinstate *Bircas Kohanim* into the daily prayers, but was arrested by government agents [on a trumped up charge unrelated to the subject at hand] before he could carry out his intention. *Vilna Gaon* interpreted this as a sign from Heaven that he was not to tamper with the prevailing custom. At a later date, *Netziv* continues, R' Chaim of Volozhin decided that the very next day he would institute daily *Bircas Kohanim* in his synagogue. That night, however, a fire spread through half the city and the synagogue was razed. Such events convinced the great men of the period that a change in the custom was contrary to God's will, except in *Eretz Yisrael (Teshuvos Meishiv Davar)*.

□ **On the Sabbath.** *Mishnah Berurah* (128:165) rules that *Bircas Kohanim* should be recited on festivals whether they fall on a Sabbath or on weekdays. Although some communities omit *Bircas Kohanim* on festivals which fall on the Sabbath, he rejects this as an improper custom.

Nevertheless, the custom is not without justification. It is based on the generally accepted custom that *Kohanim* immerse themselves in a *mikveh* on the day before a festival so that they can pronounce *Bircas Kohanim* in a state of ritual purity. Although lack of such immersion does not disqualify a *Kohen (ibid.)*, the custom is most commendable.

In order to maintain himself in this state of purity, the *Kohen* would have to refrain from conjugal relations on the evening of *Yom Tov*. On the Sabbath when such restraint is improper, the *Kohen* would not be ritually pure in the morning, when it would not always be possible to immerse himself again. This may be why many communities omitted *Bircas Kohanim* on festivals that fell on the Sabbath.

It should be noted, however, that immersion is nearly always possible on the Sabbath and, in any case, neither conjugal relations prior to *Bircas Kohanim* nor *Bircas Kohanim* without immersion are forbidden *(Sha'ar HaTziun 128:132)*.

The *Ribono Shel Olam* and *Yehi Ratzon* prayers are omitted on the Sabbath when it is forbidden to pray for personal needs.

◦§ Aspects of the Ritual

◦§ Bircas Kohanim in Shemoneh Esrei

The Talmud *(Megillah 17b-18a)* traces the development of the שְׁמֹנֶה עֶשְׂרֵה, *Shemoneh Esrei* [lit., eighteen] blessings of the *Amidah:* 'One hundred and twenty elders[1], among them many prophets, instituted the order of the *Shemoneh Esrei.*' The Talmud then lists all the blessings until the thanksgiving blessing [מוֹדִים], and continues, 'On what basis did they place *Bircas Kohanim* after the thanksgiving blessing? They followed the implication of the verse [which describes the *Bircas Kohanim* on Aaron's first day of performing the priestly functions]: *And Aaron raised his hands toward the nation and he blessed them; then he descended — having offered the sin offering, burnt offering and peace offering (Leviticus 9:22).*' The objection is then raised that this verse implies that *Bircas Kohanim* should follow the blessing for the return of Temple service [רְצֵה — which *precedes* the thanksgiving blessing]. The Talmud replies that the blessings for the Temple service and of thanksgiving blessing are considered as one [since both are forms of serving and expressing gratitude to the Omnipresent *(Rashi)*]. Thus, in effect, *Bircas Kohanim* follows רְצֵה.

When the *chazzan* in his repetition of *Shemoneh Esrei* reaches *Bircas Kohanim*, he must scrupulously set his thought to pronouncing a heartfelt blessing upon the holy nation ... Woe unto him who would seek favor before his Master while his heart is far off ... *(Zohar Chadash 40c)*. It should thus be of prime concern to the *chazzan* that he enunciate each word distinctly and not run one word into another, otherwise the blessing would be reduced to a meaningless jumble of syllables. For example, if the words פָּנָיו אֵלֶיךָ, *His face to you,* were pronounced carelessly, it would sound like פְּנָבִילְךָ, which is meaningless gibberish. Indeed, such a pronouncement would fall into the category described by the Prophet *(Isaiah 1:12)*: מִי־בִקֵּשׁ זֹאת מִיֶּדְכֶם, *Who requested this of your hands,* רְמֹס חֲצֵרָי, *to trample My courtyards* [for to distort the words of a blessing is like trampling the precincts of the Temple]. But *if the chazzan* is careful in reciting the blessing he is included

---

1. *Rambam* (Introduction to *Mishneh Torah;* see also *Hil. Tefillah* 11:4) describes this august body as the *beis din* (rabbinical court) of Ezra, whose members were known collectively as the אַנְשֵׁי כְּנֶסֶת הַגְּדוֹלָה [*Anshei Knesses HaGedolah*], *Men of the Great Assembly.* In addition to Ezra, who was the first *Kohen Gadol* of the Second Temple, *Rambam* identifies eleven individuals who belonged to this body: Chaggai, Zechariah and Malachi [the last three of the Prophets — see *Ezra* 5:1]; Daniel and his three companions, Chananiah, Mishael, and Azariah; Nechemiah, Mordechai-Bilshan and Zerubavel [see *Ezra* 2:2 — *Rashi (Avos* 1:1) includes Serayah and Re'eilayah who are also mentioned in this verse]; and Shimon HaTzaddik, who succeeded Ezra as *Kohen Gadol* [see p. 36].

among those of whom Scripture (ibid. 54:17) says: זֹאת נַחֲלַת עַבְדֵי ה' וְצִדְקָתָם מֵאִתִּי נְאֻם־ה', This is the heritage of the servants of HASHEM, and their right-eousness is from Me — the word of HASHEM (Yesod VeShoresh HaAvodah 5:6).]

⇜§ The Prior Blessing

The word בְּרָכָה, blessing, has several connotations. When God blesses man, it is a bestowal of health, success, and prosperity, both material and spiritual. When man blesses God, his blessing may be defined as thanksgiving, respect, praise, or prayer. And when man blesses his fellow, he expresses his wish that God bestow beneficence upon the blessed individual. [Bircas Kohanim is an example of the third category (Mishnah Berurah 128:88).]

Blessings with which man pays homage to his Creator are grouped into three categories: The first consists of בִּרְכוֹת הַנֶּהֱנִין, blessings recited in gratitude for the physical enjoyment of sustenance or pleasure, such as food, drink, or the smelling of fragrant odors. The enjoyment of His world is permitted only to those who show their appreciation by acknowledging Him as the supplier of all. A second category of 'homage' blessings contains בִּרְכוֹת הַמִּצְוֹת, blessings recited before the perfor-mance of a mitzvah — an example of this is the blessing pronounced prior to Bircas Kohanim. The third category, בִּרְכוֹת שֶׁבַח וְהוֹדָיָה, is the large group of general ex-pressions of praise, thanksgiving, homage and supplication that Rambam (Hil. Berachos 1:4) describes as 'constant reminders of God and a means of strengthening our awe of Him'. Among these are the blessing שֶׁהֶחֱיָנוּ, Who has kept us alive ..., recited by one who builds a new home or wears a new suit of clothing (The World of Prayer pp. 13-14).

The Rishonim [early codifiers of Halachah] disagree whether the prior blessing should be recited before the Kohanim turn to face the congregation, (Rambam, Tefillah 14:12) or after (Rashi, Sotah 39b). To comply with both opinions it has become customary for the Kohanim to begin the blessing while facing the Ark, turn in the middle of its recitation, and conclude the blessing while facing the congrega-tion (Mishnah Berurah 128:40). Until the words בִּקְדֻשָׁתוֹ שֶׁל אַהֲרֹן, with the holiness of Aaron, should be said facing the Ark, and the rest should be said while facing the congregation (R' Aryeh Yehudah of Modena cited in Birkei Yosef). [However, both the Frankfurt am Main and the Chabad-Lubavitch communities follow Rashi's view that the Kohanim turn to face the congregation before beginning the prior blessing.]

When the Kohanim turn — both toward the congregation at this point, and back toward the Ark at the conclusion of Bircas Kohanim — each Kohen should turn to his right [i.e., clockwise]. Since they were originally facing eastward toward the Ark, the Kohanim will turn south then west to face the people; upon completion of Bircas Kohanim, they turn north then east to face the Ark (Mishnah Berurah 128:61). This rule applies whether the Kohanim are right- or left-handed (Pri Megadim).

Unlike other mitzvos for which one person may recite the prior blessing and the other participants concentrate on the words and respond amen, here each Kohen must recite his own prior blessing (Magen Avraham citing Mabit).

Nevertheless, R' Betzalel HaKohen of Vilna records that he once spent the Sab-bath in Trieste, Italy, where the custom called for the Kohanim to ascend the duchan every Sabbath. Another custom of that community was that only one Kohen recited Bircas Kohanim while the others concentrated on his words and responded amen. As a guest, R' Betzalel was accorded the honor of pronouncing the blessing (cited in Ateres Paz.)

Two Kohanim who hate each other may ascend the duchan at the same time. One may not force the other into ascending on a rotation basis for each is entitled to fulfill the *mitzvah* at every opportunity that presents itself. However, a *Kohen* who is hated by the congregation or who hates even one member of the congregation should not recite *Bircas Kohanim*. If he does he places his life in danger,[1] and should leave the synagogue before *Bircas Kohanim*. The word בְּאַהֲבָה, *with love*, is added to the prior blessing to help assure that every *Kohen* should purge hate from his heart (*Mishnah Berurah* 128:37).

◄§ Position of the Kohen's Hands

As noted above ["With Raised Hands", p. 31] the Mishnah (*Sotah* 7:2) teaches that in accordance with the verse (*Leviticus* 9:22), *And Aaron raised his hands over the people and blessed them,* the *Kohanim* raise their hands during the time they bless the nation.

The Mishnah also teaches that in the Temple all *Kohanim* (with the exception of the *Kohen Gadol* [see above p. 36]) raised their outstretched hands above their heads. *Rashi* explains that since the *Kohanim* in the Temple blessed with the Ineffable Name, the *Shechinah* rested on their fingertips. Therefore, they kept their hands high so that the *Shechinah* on their fingertips would be on a higher level than their heads.

Outside the Temple environs, where the *Shechinah* is not on the *Kohanim's* fingertips, they lift their hands only to shoulder level [perhaps to indicate the *Shechinah's* absence].

□ **The Five Apertures.** No other instructions regarding the *Kohanim's* hands are found in the Talmud. However, based upon *Zohar* and various Midrashim, the *Kohanim* have come to position their hands and fingers in a particular mode. *Shir HaShirim Rabbah* explains that the verse, [*He is*] *looking through the windows, peering through the lattices (Song of Songs* 2:9), refers to God Who stands behind the *Kohanim* and looks at Israel through the spaces between their fingers [*lattices*]. For *lattices* the verse uses the word הַחֲרַכִּים, which may also be read as two words, ה׳ חֲרַכִּים, *five apertures*. These 'five openings' are created by placing the tips or joints of the thumbs together [some authorities would separate them slightly], forming one 'aperture' between them. The remaining four fingers of each hand, are paired in groups

There are more than a dozen customs on how the Kohanim *hold their hands. All are equally valid as long as five apertures are made.*
Two are illustrated above.

of two fingers each, the forefinger held together with the middle finger, and the ring finger together with the small finger. Thus, there are two more spaces in each hand; one between the thumb and forefinger, the other between the middle and ring fingers. [See illustration.]

Kabbalistically, however, *Zohar* — which relates the ten fingers to the ten *Sefiros* [see p. 80] — teaches that no two fingers should be touching. Many *Kohanim* who wish to follow both the Midrashically-base rule that the fingers should be paired and the *Zohar's* ruling that they should be separated, hold the paired fingers a hairsbreadth apart while maintaining a wide space between the other fingers (based on *Shulchan Aruch* 128:12 with *Mishnah Berurah* and other commentaries).

1. *Zohar* (III:147b) relates the story of a *Kohen* who did not pronounce *Bircas Kohanim* lovingly. Before the blessing was concluded he had become a heap of bones. Another *Kohen* arose, raised his hands, and pronounced the blessing [lovingly] and thus rectified [the mishaps] of that day.

Some authorities hold that if a *Kohen* cannot hold his fingers in this position for the entire period of the blessing, he may close his hands while the *chazzan* reads the next word and while the congregation responds *amen* (*Mishnah Berurah* 128:43).

□ **Right over Left.** Although both hands are raised the right should be slightly higher than the left. *Beis Yosef* finds an allusion to this practice in the verse from which raising of the hands is derived. In the Torah the word for *his hands* [*and Aaron raised 'his hands' over the people (Leviticus 9:22)*] is spelled defectively, יָדָו instead of יָדָיו. Since the Torah scroll is written without vowel points, the word may also be read יָדוֹ, *his hand*, in the singular. Thus, although both hands (יָדָיו) must be raised, one of them (יָדוֹ) should be above the other. Since in most instances the Torah attributes greater holiness to the right hand (e.g., *Leviticus* 14:14) we assume here too that the right hand is raised higher. [Additionally, the attribute of Divine Mercy is represented by the right and the attribute of Divine Justice by the left. Placing the right hand above the left is a symbolic gesture, asking God to treat Israel with forgiving Mercy rather than strict Justice.]

Finally, the palms must face the ground as distinct from one who raises his hand in prayer with all five fingers pointing heavenward (*Shulchan Aruch* 128:12 with *Mishnah Berurah*).

Kedushas Levi explains the significance of this position: When one receives an object he holds his hands with the palms facing upward. But when he gives away something, the giver's palm is downward. Since the *Kohanim* are here bestowing a blessing upon the congregation, their palms are held in a giving position.

□ **Spreading the Blessing.** Upon reciting each of seven words the *Kohanim* must turn toward the south and the north to indicate that their blessings are intended not only for those standing directly in front of them but also for those on either side (*Shulchan Aruch* 128:45; *Mishnah Berurah* 128:168).[1] These words are shown here in bold face type:

יְבָרֶכְךָ ה' וְיִשְׁמְרֶךָ. יָאֵר ה' פָּנָיו אֵלֶיךָ וִיחֻנֶּךָּ. יִשָּׂא ה' פָּנָיו אֵלֶיךָ וְיָשֵׂם לְךָ שָׁלוֹם.

Shulchan Aruch does not specify whether the *Kohanim* turn their hands or their faces. In most communities the *Kohanim* turn their *hands* to the right and the left. This custom is based on Scripture's juxtaposition of Aaron's hands raised in blessing with the תְּנוּפָה, *waving*, of certain parts of the peace offering. *And the breasts and the right shank Aaron waved before HASHEM as Moses had commanded. Then Aaron raised his hands over the people and blessed them (Leviticus 9:21-22).* Baal HaTurim explains that the placement of the verses indicates that Aaron — the *Kohen* — must wave his hands to the side during *Bircas Kohanim.*

In some communities, such as Frankfurt am Main, the *Kohanim* merely turn their faces upon pronouncing these seven words, but not their hands. This custom seems to be borne out by *Pri Chadash* who writes in his explanation of the turning, 'Therefore he *turns his head* north and south …

Rama explains that each of these seven words completes a blessing. *Mishnah Berurah* elaborates: Although *Bircas Kohanim* comprises three verses of blessing, each verse actually contains two blessings. Thus, יְבָרֶכְךָ ה', *may HASHEM bless you*, and וְיִשְׁמְרֶךָ, *may He watch over you*, are reckoned as two. Similarly, יָאֵר ה' פָּנָיו אֵלֶיךָ, *may HASHEM shine his countenance upon you*, and וִיחֻנֶּךָּ, *and be gracious to*

---

1. An obvious typographic or copyist's error found in some early editions of *Shulchan Aruch* — the omission of וִיחֻנֶּךָּ and the second אֵלֶיךָ from the above seven words — has been perpetuated in many of the more recent editions. Almost every commentator discussing this passage includes both words as a matter of course. See, for example, *Mishnah Berurah* (128:170) who explains the reason for the *Kohanim* turning their heads at *seven* words, despite the fact that the list appearing in the text of *Shulchan Aruch* printed with *Mishnah Berurah* has only *five* words on it.

you, are each a complete blessing; and יִשָּׂא ה' פָּנָיו אֵלֶיךָ, *may HASHEM raise His countenance toward you,* and וְיָשֵׂם לְךָ שָׁלוֹם, *may He grant you peace,* are separate and distinct.

Magen Avraham questions *Rama's* reasoning, for the word לְךָ is part of the phrase וְיָשֵׂם לְךָ שָׁלוֹם, *may He grant you peace,* and does not conclude a blessing. Rather at each word ending with the pronominal suffix ךָ, *you* [as the object of the verb to which it is appended], the *Kohanim* turn to all the congregants in the synagogue indicating that each of them is included in the word *you.*

Magen Avraham presumably accepts *Rama's* reason, only regarding the word שָׁלוֹם, which is the conclusion of *Bircas Kohanim.* Since this word is a noun and contains no pronominal suffix *Magen Avraham's* reason cannot apply. Alternatively, the words לְךָ שָׁלוֹם, [*to*] *you peace,* together form the conclusion of the blessing, for each blessing ends with a pronoun. Therefore the *Kohanim* must turn to the sides for each of these words (*Machatzis HaShekel;* cf. *Pri Chadash*).

□ **Looking at the Kohen's Hands.** While the *Kohanim* are blessing, the people should not look at them or otherwise interrupt their concentration on the *Kohanim's* words. Rather they should look downward as when praying [for *Bircas Kohanim* is in reality a prayer that God bless the nation (*Levush Mordechai*)]. Their faces should be toward the *Kohanim* but they may look neither at the *Kohen's* face nor at his hands (*Shulchan Aruch, Orach Chaim* 128:23). *Rama* adds: Likewise the *Kohanim* may not look at their own hands. Thus it has become customary for the *Kohanim* to cover their faces with the *tallis.* Some drape the tallis over their fingers to prevent the congregation from looking at them, while others extend their fingers outside of the tallis. *Mishnah Berurah* (128:92) comments that the congregation has also adopted the custom of covering their faces with the tallis during *Bircas Kohanim.*

The reason for not looking at the *Kohen's* hands when they are raised in blessing is to prevent one from concentrating on the positioning and movement of the *Kohen's* fingers instead of on the words of the blessing. Certainly one may not look elsewhere [except into his *siddur*]. Additionally, during the Temple era, when the *Kohanim* articulated the Ineffable Name during their pronouncement of *Bircas Kohanim,* the *Shechinah* ["Divine Presence"] rested on their finger tips and it would be disrespectful for the masses to look upon the *Shechinah.* Consequently, it was then forbidden to take even a quick glance at their hands. Nowadays, in the absence of the *Shechinah,* only staring prolonged enough to interrupt concentration is strictly forbidden. A glimpse, however, would technically be permitted. Nevertheless, in remembrance of the Holy Temple it is customary to avoid totally looking at the *Kohen's* hands (*Mishnah Berurah* 128:89).

⋖§ Supplication Regarding Dreams

Between the verses of *Bircas Kohanim* it is customary to recite a supplication regarding dreams. The currently prevalent version of this supplication is virtually unchanged from the text appearing in the Talmud. There it appears with the following introduction:

If one had a dream but is uncertain of what he saw [i.e., he is not sure whether the dream forebode good or evil (*Rosh*)] let him stand before the *Kohanim* at the time they spread their hands in blessing, and let him say, ... רִבּוֹנוֹ שֶׁל עוֹלָם, *Master of the world! I am Yours and my dreams are Yours* ... (Berachos 55b).[1]

---

1. In connection with the dreams that played key parts in Joseph's life, the *Overview* to *Vayeishev* [ArtScroll *Genesis* Vol. V] deals at length with the phenomena of dreams. The following is extracted from there.

A general outline of man's ability to assimilate heavenly messages in his dreams is given by

This Talmudic dictum, in turn, is based on the Midrashic interpretation of the following verse:

> Behold! The couch of Shlomo! Sixty mighty ones round about it, of the mighty ones of Israel. All gripping the sword, learned in warfare, each with his sword on his thigh, from fear in the nights. (Song of Songs 3:7-8)

Behold! The couch of Shlomo — Shlomo refers to God, because He is the Master of Shalom [peace] ...

Sixty mighty ones round about it — God's *couch* is figuratively surrounded by the sixty letters contained in *Bircas Kohanim;*

of the mighty ones of Israel — for the blessings strengthen Israel ...

All gripping the sword, learned in warfare — these blessings protect Israel against all retributions mentioned in the Torah.

Each with his sword on his thigh, from fear in the nights — if one dreams that a sword is cutting the flesh from his thigh, he should hurry to the synagogue and stand before the *Kohanim* to hear their blessing. Then no evil will befall him *(Bamidbar Rabbah 11:3)*.

[The connection between Bircas Kohanim and dreams is not clearly defined. The following possibility has been suggested. Generally speaking, minimal traces of forbidden substances are, under certain conditions, בָּטֵל בְּשִׁשִּׁים, *negated by sixty*, i.e., if a forbidden substance is mixed with a permitted substance containing sixty times

---

Derech Hashem (3:1). Sometimes God conveys a prophecy in a dream. Such prophecies come directly from God and are always fulfilled. There are other forms of metaphysical communication, however, that are received in dreams.

In addition to the soul that gives man the ability to live — a soul that is more or less similar to the lifeforce of all animals — man has a higher soul. Its function is to provide a bridge between man's animal nature and the wholly spiritual forces above him. Naturally, this soul becomes substantially limited as long as it is connected to its human host, but certain facets of it retain the power to soar above the body, so to speak, and absorb spiritual messages that ordinarily would be beyond a person's ability to comprehend. An illustration of this is found in *Megillah* 3a, which tells of Daniel who was shown a vision. His companions did not see the vision but they became frightened nonetheless. Why did they fear something of which they were unaware? asks the Talmud. Although they could not see, their 'mazal' saw (a facet of their higher soul that was capable of knowing, and fearing, what its human body could not perceive).

Night time, when a person sleeps, provides the imagination freedom from the discipline man imposes on it while he is awake and in need of all his faculties. Then people dream. They may dream of many things, most of them outgrowths of their experiences and ambitions of the day.

Another thing happens during those sleeping hours. A portion of the higher soul leaves the body and associates with spiritual beings that are unencumbered by a body. It can be told things by them, sometimes by holy angels and sometimes by evil demons. If the soul transmits these messages and revelations to man's lower intelligence, they may take the form of dreams.

Thus, dreams are of various origins. Sometimes they are pure fantasies affected by a person's health, strivings or preoccupations; such dreams have no meaning or value, except to the extent that they reveal what goes on in the individual dreamer's fantasy. If a dream reflects the message of a demon, it, too, is false. But if its origin is the teaching of a higher spiritual being, then its message is true and it is God's way of communicating knowledge of the future or insight into the present.

Since man has an active imagination, however, all dreams, even those that originate from higher sources, become intermixed with his personal images. As a result, there is no dream without some meaningless portions, and even the dreams that are essentially true will not be accurate in every detail; the parts that are realized were supplied to the higher soul by spiritual forces, while the parts that never happen were products of the dreamer's personal fantasy *(Berachos* 55a). R' Bachya (Bereishis 41:1) describes this form of revelation figuratively as נְבוּאָה קְטַנָּה, *minor prophecy;* it is what the Sages describe as חֲלוֹם אֶחָד מִשִּׁשִּׁים בִּנְבוּאָה, *a dream is one sixtieth of a prophecy (Berachos* 57a). [See the full Overview for a more complete discussion of the topic and the sources.]

its volume, then under certain conditions that prohibition may be waived. By analogy, the evil אוֹת, *omen*, of a dream, can be countered and negated by the sixty letters (the word אוֹת can mean both *omen* and *letter*) of *Bircas Kohanim*. (*Cf. Noam Elimelech, Terumah*.)]

Regarding this supplication, *Shulchan Aruch* (*Orach Chayim* 130:1) cites verbatim the Talmudic passage quoted above. *Rama* adds that if someone has had a disturbing dream on a day when the *Kohanim* do not ascend the *duchan*, this supplication should be recited while the *chazzan* recites the prayer [*Our God and the God of our forefathers* ...] in which he recites the verses of *Bircas Kohanim* and *Sim Shalom*. The supplicant should complete the supplication simultaneously with the *chazzan's* conclusion of *Sim Shalom* so that the congregational *amen* will refer to his prayer as well. If he finishes earlier than the *chazzan*, he should add the short prayer אַדִּיר בַּמָּרוֹם, *Mighty One on high* [see p. 86]. *Mishnah Berurah* (130:1) points out that in communities where the *Kohanim* ascend the *duchan* only on festivals, everyone should recite the supplication, for he has surely had at least one dream during the many weeks between festivals. *Be'ur Halachah* cautions, however, that on the second day of a festival, one who did not dream the previous night should omit the opening clause, 'I have had a dream but do not know what it indicates'. Unless he dreamt that night, the statement would be inaccurate. As for the many dreams he had in preceding weeks — they were already included in the first festival day's supplication.

◆§ The Divine Name of Twenty-two Letters

[Scripture uses many appellations for God. Each of these Divine Names represents an attribute by which God allows man to perceive Him. יְ־הֹ־וָ־ה represents the attribute of Divine Kindness. Since this Name is composed of the letters of הָיָה הֹוֶה יִהְיֶה, *He was, He is, He will be*, it is also an indication of God's Eternality. אֱלֹהִים, ELOHIM, represents Divine Justice. This word can also mean *judge* and *power*. Similarly, each Name found in Scripture is but an allusion to a different Divine attribute. Kaballah records many Divine Names which are not found explicitly in Scripture but may be derived through various Kaballistic principles. One of the Names is described in Kabbalistic literature as the twenty-two letter Name, and the letters of *Bircas Kohanim* are said to allude to it.]

R' Moshe Cordovero [*Ramak*] explains that this Twenty-two Letter Name comprises four individual Names [אנקת"ם פסי"ם פספסי"ם דיונסי"ם], each capable of effecting the fulfillment of a particular human need. The first Name, אנקת"ם, — a contraction of אֶנְקַת תְּמִים, literally *the cry of the perfect ones* — is efficacious in making one's prayer accepted in Heaven; the second, פסת"ם, is the Name through which God distributes פְּסַת בַּר, *portions of bread*, to the hungry; through the Name פספסי"ם[1] — related to כְּתֹנֶת פַּסִים, *woolen tunic*, that Jacob made for Joseph (*Genesis* 37:3) — He clothes the naked; and דיונסי"ם indicates that He performs נִסִּים, *miracles*, and wonders. These four Names were invoked by Jacob when he prayed (*Genesis* 28:21) that *God be with me and guard me on this way which I am going; and give me bread to eat and clothes to wear; and that I return in peace* ... (*Pardes*, cited in *Siddur Amudei Shamayim*).

Ramak describes the intricate manner by which this Name is derived from the letters of *Bircas Kohanim*:

---

1. In the Mishnah (*Negaim* 11:7) the word פַּסְפָּסִים refers to a multicolored garment, variously described as striped, spotted, or checked with areas of different hues. The word is derived from פַּס, the Aramaic equivalent of the Hebrew כַּף, *palm of the hand* [see *Daniel* 5:5], and alludes to the width of the patches of color on the garment (*Rav*). [Perhaps the appearance of the word פַּס three times within the twenty-two letter Name — פסי"ם פספסי"ם — is an allusion to the tripartite nature of the blessing recited with raised פַּסִים, *palms*.]

Each letter of the Hebrew alphabet has a numeric value. The nine letters א through ט represent the units from 1 through 9, respectively; from י until צ the letters are valued from 10 to 90; and the four letters ק to ת represent 100 to 400. Sometimes the 'final' letters, i.e., the five letters which take a different form at the end of a word, are reckoned independently of their regular forms, yielding: ך (final *chaf*) = 500; ם (final *mem*) = 600; ן (final *nun*) = 700; ף (final *fei*) = 800; and ץ (final *tzadi*) = 900.

Kabbalah and the Talmud (*Shabbos* 104a) teach that other orderings of the alphabet are also valid. In these orderings, the letters are arranged in sets of either two or three letters, the components of each set being interchangeable in any given word. Illustrations of this concept will be given below. For an understanding of the way in which the twenty-two letter Divine Name is derived from the verses of *Bircas Kohanim* a knowledge of five variant alphabets is necessary. (For simplicity's sake, each alphabet is named for its first two sets of letters.)

☐ א"ת-ב"ש. In this alphabet, the letters are assorted in pairs from the opposite ends of the *aleph-beis. Thus, the first letter* א is paired with the last letter ת, forming the couplet א"ת; the second letter ב, is paired with ש, the second from the last letter, forming the couplet ב"ש; the third letter ג, is paired with ר, the third from the last, ר, yielding ג"ר. This continues until eleven couplets are formed. An example of its use is the occasional Scriptural reference (*Jeremiah* 25:26 and 51:41) to בָּבֶל, *Babylon*, as שֵׁשַׁךְ, *Sheishach* — in the א"ת-ב"ש alphabet, ב is paired with ש and ל with כ. Similarly the land of כַּשְׂדִּים becomes לֵב קָמַי (*Jeremiah* 51:1).

☐ א"ב-ג"ד is composed of eleven pairs of adjacent letters: א with ב; ג with ד; ה with ו; and so on.

☐ א"ל-ב"ם is arranged by dividing the *aleph-beis* into two equal parts, one consisting of the first eleven letters, the other of the last eleven. The first letters of the two parts are paired to form the couplet א"ל, the next pair forms ב"ם, the third ג"ן etc.

☐ אח"ס-בט"ע is similar to א"ל-ב"ם but instead of two parts, the *aleph-beis* is divided into three groups of seven letters. The first letters of each group form the triplet אח"ס, the second letters בט"ע, the next letters גי"ף, etc. In this alphabet, ת, the twenty-second letter, is appended to the last set, giving it the four letters, זנש"ת.

☐ אי"ק-בכ"ר is also arrived at by a tripartite division of the alphabet. In this version however the five 'final' letters are added to the twenty-two regular letters, giving a twenty-seven letter alphabet. Splitting these letters into three nine letter groupings and taking the initial letter of each group yields אי"ק, the second letters form בכ"ר, the third גל"ש etc. This alphabet has the unique feature that all members of any given triplet have an equal מִסְפָּר קָטָן, *minor count* (a system of *gematria* in which the zero is omitted from each number, thus 2 = 20 = 200).

The full array of each of these five alphabets is presented on the following chart:

אי"ק-בכ"ר	אח"ס-בט"ע	א"ל-ב"ם	א"ב-ג"ד	א"ת-ב"ש
א=י=ק	א=ח=ס	א=ל	א=ב	א=ת
ב=כ=ר	ב=ט=ע	ב=מ	ג=ד	ב=ש
ג=ל=ש	ג=י=פ	ג=נ	ה=ו	ג=ר
ד=מ=ת	ד=כ=צ	ד=ס	ז=ח	ד=ק
ה=נ=ך	ה=ל=ק	ה=ע	ט=י	ה=צ
ו=ס=ם	ו=מ=ר	ו=פ	כ=ל	ו=פ
ז=ע=ן	ז=נ=ש=ת	ז=צ	מ=נ	ז=ע
ח=פ=ף		ח=ק	ס=ע	ח=ס
ט=צ=ץ		ט=ר	פ=צ	ט=נ
		י=ש	ק=ר	י=מ
		כ=ת	ש=ת	כ=ל

Using these five alphabets, *Ramak* elicits the Twenty-two Letter Name from the first twenty-two letters of *Bircas Kohanim*. [Although it is evident that if a long enough series of exchanges is permitted any given letter may be transformed into any other letter, *Ramak* limits each of the twenty-two letters to either one or two exchanges.] The following chart shows the appropriate transformations:

Zohar (III:147a) attaches another significance to the Twenty-two Letter Name alluded to here. After Israel sinned with the Golden Calf, only Moses' impassioned pleas for Divine mercy saved the nation from destruction. As a result of Moses' defense of Israel, God granted him a new revelation — the Thirteen Attributes of Divine Mercy (see *Exodus* 34:6-7). After the slanderous report of the spies who scouted the land of Canaan, Moses invoked Divine foregiveness with an abridged formula comprising only nine attributes (see *Numbers* 14:18). [A lengthy discussion of these two passages may be found in ArtScroll

י in אי״ק-בכ״ר becomes	א					א
ב in אח״ס-בט״ע becomes ט which in א״ת-ב״ש becomes	נ-א					נ
ד in א״ב-ג״ד becomes	ק					ק
כ in א״ל-ב״ם becomes	ת					ת
כ in א״ל-ב״ם becomes ת which in אי״ק-בכ״ר becomes	ם					ם
י in אח״ס-בט״ע becomes	פ					פ
ד in א״ב-ג״ד becomes ו which in אי״ק-בכ״ר becomes	ס					ס
ו in אח״ס-בט״ע becomes מ which in אי״ק-בכ״ר becomes	ת					ת
ד in א״ב-ג״ד becomes ו which in אח״ס-בט״ע becomes	ם					ם
ו in א״ל-ב״ם becomes	פ					פ
י in א״ת-ב״ש becomes מ which in אי״ק-בכ״ר becomes	ס					ס
ש in א״ל-ב״ם becomes י which in אח״ס-בט״ע becomes	פ					פ
מ in אי״ק-בכ״ר becomes	ס					ס
ד in אח״ס-בט״ע becomes מ which in א״ת-ב״ש becomes	י					י
ד in א״ל-ב״ם becomes ת which in אי״ק-בכ״ר becomes	ם					ם
י in א״ת-ב״ש becomes מ which in אי״ק-בכ״ר becomes	ד					ד
א in אי״ק-בכ״ר becomes	י					י
ד in אח״ס-בט״ע becomes	ו					ו
י in א״ב-ג״ד becomes ט which in א״ת-ב״ש becomes	נ					נ
ה in א״ב-ג״ד becomes ו which in אי״ק-בכ״ר becomes	ס					ס
ו in א״ת-ב״ש becomes פ which in אח״ס-בט״ע becomes	י					י
ה in א״ב-ג״ד becomes ו which in אח״ס-בט״ע becomes	ם					ם

Tashlich, pp. 16-22.] Considering the attributes of each list as distinct from the other, *Zohar* speaks of a total of Twenty-Two Divine Attributes of Mercy. These attributes are invoked by the Twenty-two Letter Name associated with *Bircas Kohanim*.

The number twenty-two is significant to *Bircas Kohanim* in another way also related to the Divine Name. The Talmud (*Succah* 45a) refers to God with the obscure term אֲנִי וָהוֹ, *Ani Vaho*[1]. *Rashi* there identifies these words as two in a series of seventy-two Names of God, each containing three letters. The complete series is composed of the letters in the three verses (*Exodus* 14:19-21), each of which contains exactly seventy-two letters. In the mystical formula by which these Names are formed, verses 19 and 21 are read in their proper order while verse 20 is read backwards. A table showing these groups of seventy-two letters is given below. From this table it may readily be seen that אֲנִי and וָהוֹ are the first and the thirty-seventh triplets of the series.

A glance at the twenty-second set of three letters reveals the Name ייי which is formed by the initial letters of the three verses of *Bircas Kohanim*, וִיבָרֶכְךָ יָאֵר יִשָׂא (R' Chaim Paltiel).[2]

---

1. [For a discussion on the significance of these terms see ArtScroll Mishnah *Succah* 4:5 and ArtScroll *Hoshanos* pp. 84-85.]

2. *Zohar* (III:147a) also makes reference to the trebled י of *Bircas Kohanim*.

✒ Minimal Kavanos

The implications of *Bircas Kohanim* that are pointed out in Midrashic and Kabbalistic literature are both many and profound. Worthy indeed is the *Kohen* capable of fully understanding and keeping in mind all the כַּוָּנוֹת [*kavanos*], *intentions*, given by such luminaries as *Arizal*. But every *Kohen* should bear in mind at least certain minimal *kavanos* as he pronounces his blessings. In general he must think of his words as an all-encompassing and bountiful blessing of life, children, and sustenance; and he must give the *brachah* lovingly. The *siddurim* offer varying lists of specific areas on which the *Kohen* should concentrate as he pronounces the appropriate phrases. A sampling of three of these is given on the chart below.

Nehora HaShalem	Amudei Shamayim	Vilna Gaon	
May HASHEM grant each of you wisdom ...	May HASHEM increase your offspring and your possessions ...	May HASHEM grant you wisdom ...	יְבָרֶכְךָ ה'
... and offspring;	... and protect them from harm.	... and prosperity	וְיִשְׁמְרֶךָ
May HASHEM grant each of you longevity ...	May HASHEM brighten His angry countenance, thereby transforming His attribute of Judgment to His attribute of Mercy ...	May HASHEM grant you life ...	יָאֵר ה' פָּנָיו אֵלֶיךָ
... and favor in His eyes and in the eyes of your fellow men;	... and favor you, even if you are unworthy.	... and honor, so that you are never subservient to another	וִיחֻנֶּךָּ
May HASHEM grant each of you wealth ...	May HASHEM act favorably toward you ...	May HASHEM grant you children ...	יִשָּׂא ה' פָּנָיו אֵלֶיךָ
... and peace.	... and grant you peace, the only vessel capable of containing unlimited blessing.	... and peace.	וְיָשֵׂם לְךָ שָׁלוֹם

&§ III. Order of Bircas Kohanim

&§ IV. Laws of Bircas Kohanim

During the chazzan's recital of רְצֵה, the Kohanim ascend the duchan and stand facing the Ark. If they have not yet finished washing their hands, the chazzan should wait for them before beginning רְצֵה.

רְצֵה יהוה אֱלֹהֵינוּ בְּעַמְּךָ יִשְׂרָאֵל וּבִתְפִלָּתָם.
וְהָשֵׁב אֶת הָעֲבוֹדָה לִדְבִיר בֵּיתֶךָ, וְאִשֵּׁי
יִשְׂרָאֵל וּתְפִלָּתָם בְּאַהֲבָה תְקַבֵּל בְּרָצוֹן, וּתְהִי
לְרָצוֹן תָּמִיד עֲבוֹדַת יִשְׂרָאֵל עַמֶּךָ:

The following is said by the congregation and Kohanim and is repeated by the chazzan.

וְתֶעֱרַב עָלֶיךָ עֲתִירָתֵנוּ כְּעוֹלָה וּכְקָרְבָּן.
אָנָּא, רַחוּם, בְּרַחֲמֶיךָ הָרַבִּים הָשֵׁב

◆§ רְצֵה — Be Favorable

When the *chazzan* begins the blessing of רְצֵה ["Be Favorable"] every *Kohen* in the synagogue should move from his place toward the *duchan*. Even if he does not reach there until the *chazzan* finishes the next blessing he may ascend (*SA* 8; *MB* 27). If, however, he did not move when the *chazzan* began רְצֵה, he may make his way to the *duchan* as long as the *chazzan* has not finished that blessing (*MB* 25). If a *Kohen* forgot to wash his hands and the *chazzan* has already reached רְצֵה, he should nevertheless, ascend the *duchan* and water should be brought there for the washing (*MB* 27).

If a *Kohen*, in fact, did not move forward during רְצֵה, he may not ascend the *duchan*, even if the delay was beyond the *Kohen's* control (*SA* 8; *MB* 28). Therefore, upon reaching רְצֵה, the *chazzan* should pause until all the *Kohanim* have returned from washing their hands (*MB* 28).

Kohanim who do not wish to ascend the *duchan* because they are ill or weak should leave the synagogue before the *chazzan* begins רְצֵה, and should not return until after the call 'Kohanim' has been issued, but it is preferable for them to remain outside until *Bircas Kohanim* has been completed (*SA* 4; *MB* 12).

בְּעַמְּךָ יִשְׂרָאֵל וּבִתְפִלָּתָם — *Toward Your people Israel and their prayer.*

During the preceding blessings of the *Shemoneh Esrei*, we have used the second person plural: קַוֵּינוּ, *we anticipate*; תְּפִלָּתֵנוּ, *our prayer*, and so on. Why do we now change to third person and ask God to accept *their* prayer? — In this blessing we make a request that requires more merit than that possessed by the group of people with whom we are praying together. We are asking that God find favor and pleasure in our prayers. We are ashamed to suggest that *our* prayer alone is sufficiently worthy of that; we need the combined merit of all the righteous and devout people that Israel possesses. Even our earlier prayer

for forgiveness is a simpler request than this one. It is quite possible that God will forgive a sin to the extent that He will not punish the wrongdoer, but He may not find pleasure in his prayer (*Vilna Gaon*).

הָעֲבוֹדָה — *The service.*

Having come to the last part of *Shemoneh Esrei*, which is our substitute for the Temple's sacrificial service, we ask that the *true* service be restored to the Temple (*Etz Yosef*).

לִדְבִיר בֵּיתֶךָ — *To the Holy of Your Temple.*

The paramount service of the year was that of Yom Kippur, the only Temple service that was performed in the

B*e favorable, HASHEM, our God, toward Your people Israel and their prayer and restore the service to the Holy of your Temple. The fire-offerings of Israel and their prayer accept with love and favor, and may the service of Your people Israel always be pleasing to You.*

The following is said by the congregation and Kohanim and is repeated by the chazzan.

M*ay our entreaty be pleasing unto You as a burnt offering and as a sacrifice. Please, O Merciful One, in*

Holy of Holies. That sacred place is called דְּבִיר from דָּבָר, *word*, because it was from there that God's word came to Moses (*Iyun Tefillah*).

וְאִשֵׁי יִשְׂרָאֵל וּתְפִלָּתָם — *The fire-offerings of Israel and their prayer.*

The angel Michael constantly places the souls of the righteous on an altar before God, as it were, because their accomplished lives are as pleasing to Him as the sacrificial service of the Temple. Thus we pray that God always be pleased with the deeds of Israel's righteous people and their prayer (*Tosafos, Menachos* 110a, s.v. וּמיכאל;).

Alternatively: אִשֵׁי יִשְׂרָאֵל refers to the prayers of Israel, which take the place of Temple offerings. Accordingly, the phrase would be rendered: and the *fire-offerings* [i.e., the *prayers*] of Israel (*Tur Orach Chaim* 120; *Prishah*).

Or, this is a prayer for the future: May the Holy fires return to the top of the rebuilt altar (*R' Yaakov Emden*), or may the sacrifices once more be offered on the altar fires (*Avodas Yisrael*). May they and the accompanying prayers that will be offered in the Temple be accepted by You.

Tosafos and *Tur* (*ibid.*) offer a different punctuation in this blessing. According to this alternative (accepted by *Be'ur HaGra, Orach Chaim* 120), the phrase *fire-offerings of Israel* is the end of the preceding sentence: *Restore the service to the Holy of Your Temple and* [also restore] *the fire-offerings of Israel.* I.e., Restore the Yom Kippur service *to the Holy of Your Temple* and also bring back the *fire-offerings* that are brought in the outer precincts of the Temple (*Iyun Tefillah*).

◆§ וְתֶעֱרַב — **May it be Pleasing**

During the *Mussaf* service at which *Kohanim* ascend the *duchan*, two emendations of the blessing רְצֵה are customarily made by *Ashkenazim*. [In most communities these changes are not made on those occasions when the *Kohanim* ascend the *duchan* during the *Shacharis* service, such as on Simchas Torah.] When the chazzan reaches the words וְתֶחֱזֶינָה עֵינֵינוּ, *May our eyes behold ...*, the congregation and *Kohanim* recite the prayer וְתֶעֱרַב, *May (it) be pleasing;* it is then repeated by the chazzan. Additionally, the *chazzan's* conclusion of the blessing is altered.

Likutei Mahariach suggests that וְתֶעֱרַב was added to the *Shemoneh Esrei* as a signal to the *Kohanim* to ascend the *duchan*. As noted above, unless a *Kohen* steps forward during רְצֵה, he may not ascend the *duchan*. The Rabbis found it advisable, therefore, to insert a paragraph that would be recited only during a *Shemoneh Esrei* in which *Bircas Kohanim* is pronounced.

שְׁכִינָתְךָ לְצִיּוֹן עִירֶךָ, וְסֵדֶר הָעֲבוֹדָה לִירוּשָׁלָיִם. וְתֶחֱזֶינָה עֵינֵינוּ בְּשׁוּבְךָ לְצִיּוֹן בְּרַחֲמִים, וְשָׁם נַעֲבָדְךָ בְּיִרְאָה כִּימֵי עוֹלָם וּכְשָׁנִים קַדְמוֹנִיּוֹת.

The chazzan concludes:

בָּרוּךְ אַתָּה יהוה, שֶׁאוֹתְךָ לְבַדְּךָ בְּיִרְאָה נַעֲבוֹד.

וְתֶעֱרַב עָלֶיךָ עֲתִירָתֵנוּ — *May our entreaty be pleasing unto* [lit. *upon*] *You*.

The Talmud *(Succah 14a)* explains that the prayers of the righteous are compared to an עתר, an instrument used for winnowing grain. Just as this tool turns over the grain on the threshing floor, so do the prayers of the righteous cause the Holy One, Blessed is He, to change from judging mankind with His attributes of strict Justice to His attribute of Mercy. The Midrash *(Bereishis Rabbah* 63:5) adds that their prayers are capable of reversing an evil decree just as the עתר turns over the crop *(Iyun Tefillah)*.

An alternate reading found in many *siddurim* is וְתֶעֱרַב לְפָנֶיךָ עֲתִירָתֵנוּ, *May our entreaty become pleasing 'before' You.* This reading, however, is rejected by *Ibn Ezra (Tzachus)* because the root ערב, *pleasant,* is never found in Scripture with the preposition לִפְנֵי, *before,* but is usually followed by some form of עַל, *upon (Dover Shalom)*.

בְּעוֹלָה וּכְקׇרְבָּן — *As a burnt offering and as a sacrifice.*

The redundancy of *burnt offering* and *sacrifice* is explained by the commentators. *Burnt offering* refers to the עוֹלַת תָּמִיד, *daily communal burnt offering,* while *sacrifice* alludes to the מוּסָפִים, *additional offerings,* of the festivals which include both burnt offerings and a he-goat sin offering. This explains why this prayer is only recited at the *Mussaf* service. Moreover, it is only added on days when the *Kohanim* ascend the *duchan,* because of the similarity between *Bircas Kohanim* and the prayers of the righteous. Both are capable of turning Justice to Mercy; the

prayers of the righteous [see *Commentary* above, s.v. וְתֶעֱרַב עָלֶיךָ], and *Bircas Kohanim,* as the Talmud *(Jerusalem Sotah* 9:15) teaches, although God's anger is permitted to reign for a moment each day, this anger is mitigated by *Bircas Kohanim (Iyun Tefillah)*.

Alternatively, this prayer alludes to the different laws governing the disposition of burnt offerings and peace offerings. Burnt offerings are entirely burnt on the altar pyres, while peace offerings are partially consumed by the person offering them. This is analogous to two types of prayers. The truly righteous negate every aspect of their existence except for the service of their Creator. Even when praying for sustenance, the intention is not self-satisfaction, but to acquire the means by which to serve him better. Such prayers are properly likened to a burnt offering, which is placed on the altar in its entirety. But not everybody is capable of such lofty Divine service. Many serve their Creator, but want something in return. Their service is more like a peace offering, which goes partially for the altar and partially for its owner. Thus we pray that both kinds of supplication be found as pleasing and acceptable as altar sacrifices *(Dover Shalom)*.

רַחוּם — *O Merciful One.*

One of the Thirteen Attributes of Divine Mercy [*Exodus* 34:6-7] is רַחוּם, *Merciful One.* This attribute is variously defined as:

— The mercy that protects someone from harm, like a father's mercy on his son *(Ibn Ezra; Tos. Rosh Hashanah* 17b).

— The *source* of all mercy; not merely מְרַחֵם, *one who acts mercifully,* but One

Your abounding mercy return Your Shechinah to Zion, Your city, and the order of the Temple service to Jerusalem. And may our eyes behold when You return to Zion in mercy, that we may there serve You with awe as in days of old and as in earlier years. Chazzan *concludes:* **Blessed are You HASHEM, for You alone do we serve with awe.**

whose very being is Mercy *(Ramban)*.
— He is merciful on behalf of those deserving of punishment and eases the intensity of their suffering, if they call out to Him *(Sforno)*.

הָשֵׁב שְׁכִינָתְךָ לְצִיּוֹן עִירֶךָ — *Return Your Shechinah to Zion, Your city.*

[The *Shechinah*, God's presence, has exiled Itself, as it were from Jerusalem. May it once again rest there in His re-built Temple. The concept of *Shechinah* in exile is the theme of chapters 9-11 of *Ezekiel*. There, in response to the idol-worship of Israel, the *Shechinah* withdraws, first from the Temple and then from Jerusalem, presaging the destruction of the Temple and the expulsion of Israel from Jerusalem. Gradually, step by step, the *Shechinah* withdraws from its residence. For God's dwelling is not within buildings, but within hearts and minds. When they have no room for Him, He departs. Where sanctity is profaned, where purity is defiled, there the Divine Presence is not — indeed cannot be — manifest (see ArtScroll *Yechezkel*).

But after the *Shechinah* and then the entire nation are exiled from *Eretz Yisrael*, God says: *Though I have removed them far off among the nations, and though I have scattered them among the countries, yet I have been for them a small sanctuary* (מִקְדַּשׁ מְעַט) *in the countries where they came* (*Ezekiel* 11:16).

· The term מִקְדַּשׁ מְעַט, *small sanctuary*, is rendered by *Targum* as *synagogue*, meaning that the synagogue takes the place of the Temple while Israel is in ex-ile, but it is smaller, lesser, than Jerusalem's Holy Temple. Yet, God says, 'Anyone who joins in communal (i.e. synagogue) prayer is considered as

having redeemed Me and My children from among the nations of their exile' (*Berachos* 8a).

While gathered in the synagogue, we ask, therefore, for the *Shechinah's* return to Jerusalem, so that we may once again worship — not in the present *small sanctuary*, but — in the בַּיִת הַגָּדוֹל, *Great House* (see *II Chronicles* 3:5).

וְשָׁם נַעֲבָדְךָ בְּיִרְאָה כִּימֵי עוֹלָם ... לְבַדְּךָ בְּיִרְאָה נַעֲבוֹד — *That we may there serve You with awe as in days of old ... You alone do we serve with awe.*

In days of old alludes to the time of the first recorded offering when *Cain brought an offering to HASHEM of the fruit of the ground and Abel also brought of the firstlings of his flock ...* (*Genesis* 4:3-4). At that time, idolatry was still unknown [see *commentary* to *Genesis* 4:26; *Rambam, Hil. Avodas Kochavim* 1:1-2]. We pray for a return to the *days of old*, when God alone was the object of worship. Thus, the conclu-sion of the blessing, *You alone do we serve in awe,* was formulated to parallel the sentiment preceding it *(Dover Shalom)*.

שְׁאוֹתְךָ לְבַדְּךָ בְּיִרְאָה נַעֲבוֹד — *For You alone do we serve with awe.*

Many of the early commentators write that this was the conclusion of the blessing as it was recited in the Temple (e.g., *Rashi* to *Berachos* 11b and *Yoma* 68b).

The usual ending of this blessing reads הַמַּחֲזִיר שְׁכִינָתוֹ לְצִיּוֹן, *Who returns his Shechinah to Zion*. *Vilna Gaon* ob-jects to any change in the standard blessing upon the occasion of *Bircas Kohanim*, and classifies it as 'altering the formula ordained by the Talmudic Sages'.

The daily formula *who returns His*

מוֹדִים אֲנַחְנוּ לָךְ
שָׁאַתָּה הוּא
יהוה אֱלֹהֵינוּ וֵאלֹהֵי
אֲבוֹתֵינוּ לְעוֹלָם וָעֶד,
צוּר חַיֵּינוּ מָגֵן יִשְׁעֵנוּ.
אַתָּה הוּא לְדוֹר וָדוֹר.
נוֹדֶה לְךָ וּנְסַפֵּר
תְּהִלָּתֶךָ עַל חַיֵּינוּ
הַמְּסוּרִים בְּיָדֶךָ, וְעַל
נִשְׁמוֹתֵינוּ הַפְּקוּדוֹת

מוֹדִים דְּרַבָּנָן

מוֹדִים אֲנַחְנוּ לָךְ, שָׁאַתָּה
הוּא יהוה אֱלֹהֵינוּ
וֵאלֹהֵי אֲבוֹתֵינוּ. אֱלֹהֵי כָל
בָּשָׂר, יוֹצְרֵנוּ, יוֹצֵר בְּרֵאשִׁית,
בְּרָכוֹת וְהוֹדָאוֹת לְשִׁמְךָ הַגָּדוֹל
וְהַקָּדוֹשׁ עַל שֶׁהֶחֱיִיתָנוּ
וְקִיַּמְתָּנוּ. כֵּן תְּחַיֵּנוּ וּתְקַיְּמֵנוּ,
וְתֶאֱסוֹף גָּלֻיּוֹתֵינוּ לְחַצְרוֹת
קָדְשֶׁךָ לִשְׁמוֹר חֻקֶּיךָ וְלַעֲשׂוֹת
רְצוֹנֶךָ, וּלְעָבְדְּךָ בְּלֵבָב שָׁלֵם,
עַל שֶׁאֲנַחְנוּ מוֹדִים לָךְ. בָּרוּךְ
אֵל הַהוֹדָאוֹת.

Shechinah to Zion was presumably adopted after the destruction of the Second Temple. *Beis Yosef* (112) cites *Shibolei HaLeket* who records a Midrash tracing the history of each of the blessings of *Shemoneh Esrei*. When the *Shechinah* descended to the *Mishkan* [Tabernacle] in the Wilderness, the ministering angels declared, 'He returns his *Shechinah* to Zion.' *Orchos Chayim* adds that upon the return of the *Shechinah* to the Second Temple the angels pronounced the same blessing.

מוֹדִים — Modim

מוֹדִים אֲנַחְנוּ לָךְ — *We gratefully thank You.*

The Talmud (*Megillah* 18a) explains that this blessing of thanksgiving follows logically after the blessing of the Temple service, because עֲבוֹדָה וְהוֹדָאָה חֲדָא מִלְתָא הִיא, *service and thanks are in the same category.* This implies that to thank God for His graciousness without accepting the obligation to serve Him is blasphemous. How dare one acknowledge that his very existence, both personal and national, stems from God's mercy, without simultaneously accepting the obligation to do His will? (*R' Munk*)

צוּר חַיֵּינוּ — *The Rock of our lives.*

Our parents are the 'rocks' from whom our *bodies* are hewn, but from You we receive life itself (*Etz Yosef*).

נוֹדֶה לְךָ — *We shall thank You.*

Having begun the blessing by describing God's greatness and our relationship to Him, we now specify what we thank Him for.

עַל חַיֵּינוּ — *For our lives.*

Lest anyone think that he is master over his own life, we acknowledge that every breath and heartbeat are direct results of Your mercy (*Olas Tamid*).

נִשְׁמוֹתֵינוּ הַפְּקוּדוֹת לָךְ — *Our souls, that are entrusted to You.*

The word נְשָׁמָה [*neshamah*] refers to the higher soul that gives man his holiness, as opposed to the lower soul that merely keeps him alive. During sleep, the animal soul remains in man; he remains alive and his body functions. But the *neshamah* leaves the body and ascends to higher spiritual realms where it can conceivably receive Divine communications. Occasionally such messages become known to a person through dreams that may seem to be intuitive, but may be messages from on high, such as the prophetic dreams found in Scripture. During slumber, the *neshamah* leaves the body and is, so to

Order of Bircas Kohanim [54]

We gratefully thank You, for it is You who are HASHEM, our God and the God of our fathers forever. You are the Rock of our lives, the Shield of our salvation from generation to generation. We shall thank You and relate Your praise — for our lives, which is committed to Your power and our souls, that are entrusted to You, for

MODIM OF THE RABBIS

We gratefully thank You for it is You Who are HASHEM, our God and the God of our fathers, the God of all flesh, our Creator, the Creator of the universe. Blessings and thanks are due Your great and holy Name for you have given us life and sustained us. So may you continue to give us life and sustain us and gather our exiles to the Courtyards of Your Sanctuary, to observe Your decrees and do Your will and to serve you wholeheartedly. [We thank You] for inspiring us to thank You. Blessed be the God of thanksgiving.

---

speak, entrusted to God's safekeeping, to be returned to man every morning (Derech HaShem).

The Zohar teaches that if one has agreed to hold an object for its owner, he has no right to keep it on the grounds that the owner owes him money. Having accepted custody of the object on the understanding that he will return it

on demand, he may not keep it to enforce some other claim. This law is derived from the behavior of God. Although He can always claim that we 'owe' Him our lives because we have failed to honor our commitments to Him, He still returns our souls every morning (K'tzos HaChosen ch. 4).

N'siv Binah cites a different in-

⊰§ מוֹדִים דְּרַבָּנָן — Modim of the Rabbis

When the chazzan bows and recites Modim in the manner of a slave accepting the total authority of his master, the congregation must do likewise. The surrender of independence signified by Modim is not something that can be done through an agent. Although the chazzan can represent us in making requests, because everyone seeks God's blessing, no one can assume that people willingly give up their freedom. Therefore each member of the congregation must make his own declaration (Abudraham).

The Talmud (Sotah 40a and Yerushalmi 1:8) cites the personal declarations used by a number of rabbis, and concludes that the popular custom is to recite them all. It is called 'Modim of the Rabbis' because it consists of the combined statements of many rabbis and to indicate that it is not part of the service composed by אַנְשֵׁי כְּנֶסֶת הַגְּדֹלָה, Men

of the Great Assembly (Iyun Tefillah). Although the theme of all the statements is similar, each succeeding section of the Modim adds something to the preceding one (Rashi).

יוֹצֵר בְּרֵאשִׁית — The Creator of the universe. Although the literal meaning of בְּרֵאשִׁית is the beginning, it is used to mean the entire universe that was set in motion when God made the first statement of creation at the beginning of Genesis (Iyun Tefillah).

עַל שֶׁאֲנַחְנוּ מוֹדִים לָךְ — [We thank You] for inspiring us to thank You. The original version of this Modim (Sotah 40a) was מוֹדִים אֲנַחְנוּ לָךְ עַל שֶׁאֲנַחְנוּ מוֹדִים לָךְ, We gratefully thank You, for inspiring us to thank You (Rashi). Abudraham explains that we thank God for singling us out from all the nations to praise and thank Him.

לָךְ, וְעַל נִסֶּיךָ שֶׁבְּכָל יוֹם עִמָּנוּ, וְעַל נִפְלְאוֹתֶיךָ
וְטוֹבוֹתֶיךָ שֶׁבְּכָל עֵת, עֶרֶב וָבֹקֶר וְצָהֳרָיִם. הַטּוֹב
כִּי לֹא כָלוּ רַחֲמֶיךָ, וְהַמְרַחֵם כִּי לֹא תַמּוּ חֲסָדֶיךָ,
מֵעוֹלָם קִוִּינוּ לָךְ:

וְעַל כֻּלָּם יִתְבָּרַךְ וְיִתְרוֹמַם שִׁמְךָ מַלְכֵּנוּ תָּמִיד
לְעוֹלָם וָעֶד.

When the chazzan recites וְכֹל הַחַיִּים, the Kohanim יְהִי רָצוֹן. (Some non-Kohanim have also taken to saying this prayer but substitute שֶׁצִּוִּיתָ, You have commanded [the Kohanim] for שֶׁצִּוִּיתָנוּ, You have commanded us.) The supplication should be concluded simultaneously with the chazzan's conclusion of וְכֹל הַחַיִּים.

וְכֹל הַחַיִּים יוֹדוּךָ סֶּלָה, **יְהִי** רָצוֹן מִלְּפָנֶיךָ, יהוה אֱלֹהֵינוּ וְאלֹהֵי אֲבוֹתֵינוּ, שֶׁתְּהֵא הַבְּרָכָה הַזֹּאת שֶׁצִּוִּיתָנוּ לְבָרֵךְ אֶת עַמְּךָ יִשְׂרָאֵל וִיהַלְלוּ אֶת שִׁמְךָ בֶּאֱמֶת, הָאֵל יְשׁוּעָתֵנוּ וְעֶזְרָתֵנוּ סֶלָה. בָּרוּךְ אַתָּה.

terpretation by R' Yaakov Zvi Mecklenburg. *Our souls are beholden to You;* You have placed souls in our bodies because you want the soul to bring holiness into the animal body. That is our obligation to You.

נִסֶּיךָ ... נִפְלְאוֹתֶיךָ — *Your ... miracles ... Your wonders.*

In this context, *miracles* are the extraordinary events that everyone recognizes as the results of God's intervention. *Wonders* are the familiar things that we regard as normal, like breathing, raining, and growing. We are accustomed to them because they happen בְּכָל עֵת, *at all times,* so we call them 'natural phenomena' rather than miracles. Logically, however, there is no reason why oil should burn while water extinguishes fire — except that God has willed oil and water to act in different ways. In *Modim,* we thank God for both, because we know that He is their Creator (*Etz Yosef*).

טוֹב ... רַחֲמִים ... חֶסֶד — *Beneficence ... compassion ... kindness.*

The three Hebrew terms mean as fol-

lows: טוֹב, *goodness* or *beneficence,* is the kind deed that was actually done; רַחֲמִים is the *compassion* with which God softens the decision calls for by strict Justice. Thus, compassion will cause an offender to receive less than his deserved punishment, but he may well be punished to some degree; חֶסֶד, *compassion,* is God's infinite store of kindness. It can either overcome completely the dictates of Justice, or it can provide the רַחֲמִים that mitigates Justice (*R' Munk*).

וְכֹל הַחַיִּים — Everything Alive

When King Hezekiah recovered from an illness that had seemed to be terminal he said: *The grave cannot thank You, nor can the dead praise You; those who have descended to the pit cannot hope for Your truth. The living — only the living — can gratefully thank You* (Isaiah 38:18-19). Echoing Hezekiah, we proclaim that as long as there is life, people can express their thanks to God (*Etz Yosef*).

Even if we lack as much prosperity and happiness as we would like — we

Your daily miracles with us, and for Your wonders and favors at all times evening, morning, and noon. You are the Beneficent One, for Your compassions never ended and You are the Compassionate One, for Your kindness was never exhausted. Always have we put our hope in You.

For all these, may Your Name be continually blessed and exalted forever.

When the chazzan recites וְכֹל הַחַיִּים, *the Kohanim* יְהִי רָצוֹן. *(Some non-Kohanim have also taken to saying this prayer but substitute* שֶׁצִּוִּיתָ, You have commanded [the Kohanim] *for* שֶׁצִּוִּיתָנוּ, You have commanded us.) The supplication should be concluded simultaneously with the chazzan's conclusion of* וְכֹל הַחַיִּים.

Everything alive will gratefully acknowledge You and sincerely praise Your Name, the God of our salvation and help,

May it be acceptable before You, HASHEM, our God and the God of our fathers, that this blessing which You have commanded us to bestow upon

---

are still *alive* and for that we should express our gratitude (*Siach Yitzchak*).

וִיהַלְלוּ אֶת שִׁמְךָ בֶּאֱמֶת — *And sincerely praise Your Name.*

Sometimes people express gratitude in the hope that their benefactor will

give them even more. That is not our intention. We thank God in sincerity, and even when we request further generosity, we do so because it is His desire that we pray for our needs (*Olas Tamid*).

◆§ יְהִי רָצוֹן — The Kohen's Prayer

This short prayer is mentioned in the Talmud (*Sotah* 39a): When the *Kohen* moves his feet [to ascend the platform, and faces the Ark (*Rashi*)], what does he say? — May it be acceptable before You, HASHEM, our God, regarding this blessing [with] which You have commanded us to bless Your nation Israel, that it contain neither stumbling block nor sin.

The version now used contains some additional phrases that do not appear in the Talmud: *a full blessing* and *from now and forever.* These insertions do appear, however, in *Rambam* (*Tefillah* 14:12). The phrase *and the God of our fathers* appears neither in the Talmud nor in *Rambam*.

Present day custom calls for this prayer to be recited following *Modim DeRabbanan,* and the Kohen should time his conclusion of this prayer to coincide with the *chazzan's* ending of the congregational *amen* so it will be in response to their prayer as well as the *chazzan's* (*Rashi, Sotah* 39b; *Mishnah Berurah* 128:30).

וֵאלֹהֵי אֲבוֹתֵינוּ — *And the God of our fathers.*

The invocation of ·the God of our fathers here appears neither in the Talmud nor in *Rambam*. It is based on the Midrash (*Bamidbar Rabbah* 43:8;

cited on p. 27), which teaches that Israel is worthy of *Bircas Kohanim* in the merit of the Patriarchs (*R' Yehudah ben Yakar*).

בְּרָכָה שְׁלֵמָה — *A full blessing.*

May we [the *Kohanim*] be worthy of

יהוה הַטּוֹב שִׁמְךָ וּלְךָ נָאֶה בְּרָכָה שְׁלֵמָה, וְלֹא יִהְיֶה
בָּהּ שׁוּם מִכְשׁוֹל וְעָוֹן
לְהוֹדוֹת: מֵעַתָּה וְעַד עוֹלָם.

The chazzan recites the following in an undertone but says the word כֹּהֲנִים
aloud as the formal summons to the Kohanim, then continues in an undertone.
In some communities the congregation, but not the Kohanim, responds עַם
קְדוֹשֶׁךָ כָּאָמוּר aloud.

אֱלֹהֵינוּ וֵאלֹהֵי אֲבוֹתֵינוּ, בָּרְכֵנוּ בַבְּרָכָה הַמְשֻׁלֶּשֶׁת
בַּתּוֹרָה, הַכְּתוּבָה עַל יְדֵי מֹשֶׁה עַבְדֶּךָ,
הָאֲמוּרָה מִפִּי אַהֲרֹן וּבָנָיו,

issuing a whole-hearted blessing, as
Sifre expounds on the verse (Deuteronomy 11:13) וּלְעָבְדוֹ בְּכָל לְבַבְכֶם, and to
serve Him with all your hearts — this is
an adominition to the Kohanim that
their hearts [i.e., their intentions] be
שָׁלֵם, full, at the time of their service (R'
Yehudah ben Yakar).

וְלֹא יִהְיֶה בָּהּ שׁוּם מִכְשׁוֹל וְעָוֹן — That there
be in it neither stumbling block nor sin.
Stumbling block refers to either a slip
of the tongue or a mistake in wording;
sin pertains to those iniquities which
prohibit a Kohen from pronouncing
Bircas Kohanim (Amudei Shamayim;
see pp. 94-95).
R' Yehudah ben Yakar explains that
the plea that the blessing contain no sin
is related to the earlier prayer that the

blessing be 'full'. The first word of
Bircas Kohanim, וְיִשְׁמְרֶךָ, and may He
watch over you, is interpreted by Sifre
as a blessing that the people be
protected from Gehinnom. But if the
Kohanim are guilty of sin, then they
themselves will not be protected from
Gehinnom — and consequently their
blessing will be incomplete, because
they cannot give what they themselves
lack.

מֵעַתָּה וְעַד עוֹלָם — From now and
forever.
If there is no sin now there will be no
sin later, for as the Mishnah teaches
(Avos 4:2): מִצְוָה גוֹרֶרֶת מִצְוָה, one mitzvah brings another in its wake (Amudei
Shamayim).

בָּרְכֵנוּ בַבְּרָכָה — Summons to the Kohanim

Having ascended the duchan during the chazzan's recital of רְצֵה, the Kohanim
stand facing the Ark, their backs to the congregation, until the chazzan concludes
מוֹדִים. They do not yet raise their hands (Orach Chaim 128:10). The prevalent practice in most communities is for the chazzan to recite in an undertone the short introductory prayer ... אֱלֹהֵינוּ וֵאלֹהֵי אֲבוֹתֵינוּ בָּרְכֵנוּ 'Our God ... bless us ... 'until the
word כֹּהֲנִים, Kohanim, which he calls out in a loud voice. Then, resuming his undertone, he recites the next words עַם קְדוֹשֶׁךָ כָּאָמוּר, 'Your holy people, as it is said.'
[In many communities the congregation, excluding the Kohanim, recites these three
words aloud in response to the chazzan's call.] Even if only one Kohen is present,
the chazzan uses the word Kohanim in plural, since it is the established form of the
prayer. In some communities the chazzan merely calls out Kohanim without
reciting the introductory prayer. In these places the chazzan announces Kohanim
only if two or more Kohanim ascend the duchan. If only one Kohen is present,
however, he does not wait for a call, but begins his blessing immediately (Mishnah
Berurah 128:38).

selah! Blessed are You, HASHEM, Your Name is the Beneficial One and to You it is seemly to give thanks.

Your nation Israel be a full blessing, that there be in it neither stumbling block nor sin from now and forever.

The chazzan recites the following in an undertone but says the word כֹּהֲנִים aloud as the formal summons to the Kohanim, then continues in an undertone. In some communities the congregation, but not the Kohanim, responds עַם קְדוֹשֶׁךָ כָּאָמוּר aloud.

Our God and the God of our fathers, bless us with the blessing that is trebled in the Torah, written by the hand of Moses Your servant, and spoken by the mouth of Aaron and his sons,

אֱלֹהֵינוּ וַאלֹהֵי אֲבוֹתֵינוּ — *Our God and the God of our fathers.*

[See commentary above, s.v. וַאלֹהֵי אֲבוֹתֵינוּ.]

בָּרְכֵנוּ בַבְּרָכָה — *Bless us with the blessing.*

[We ask God, not the *Kohanim* to bless us, because, although the *Kohanim* pronounce the words, they are merely conduits through which the blessing descends from God to the nation below — as the Talmud (*Chullin* 49a) teaches: וַאֲנִי אֲבָרְכֵם, *And I shall bless them* (*Numbers* 6:27), implies that God, Himself, is the source of the blessing. Thus, pray: *Our God ... bless us.*]

בְּרָכָה הַמְשֻׁלֶּשֶׁת בַּתּוֹרָה — *The blessing that is trebled in the Torah.*

Trebled in the Torah does not mean that the verses of *Bircas Kohanim* are to be found in the Torah three times — they appear only once. What the phrase alludes to is the Talmudic dictum (*Berachos* 8a) that each person should review the weekly Torah portion three times — twice in the original wording of the verse and once in the Targumic translation. But the Mishnah (*Megillah* 4:10) teaches that *Bircas Kohanim* should not be translated in the *Targum*[1]. Therefore to fulfill his

obligation of thrice reviewing the portion one must read the verses of *Bircas Kohanim* all three times as they appear in the Torah. Thus, the expression *trebled in the Torah* (*Shlah* cited by *Etz Yosef*).

Alternatively, הַמְשֻׁלֶּשֶׁת may be translated *threefold,* for each of *Bircas Kohanim*'s three verses is a separate blessing (see Mishnah *Sotah* 7:6 and *Tamid* 7:2). These three blessings correspond to the three Patriarchs: Abraham, Isaac and Jacob (*Chomas Anach;* see above p. 27). *Pri Tzaddik* refers to the Patriarchs with the verse from *Ecclesiastes* (4:12), *The three-ply cord is not easily severed.* Jacob, the third of the Patriarchs, combined Abraham's virtue of חֶסֶד, *kindness,* with Israel's personification of גְבוּרָה, *power,* into an unbreakable cord of תִּפְאֶרֶת, *splendor* [see below pp. 80-81]. Thus, Jacob is called בְּחִיר הָאָבוֹת, *the chosen one among the Patriarchs,* because he combined the virtues of Abraham and Isaac with his own — *the three-ply cord* — making their heritage eternal. [This thought corresponds to the Mishnah's dictum (*Uktzin* 3:12) that God found no utensil more suitable for containing blessing then שָׁלוֹם, *peace.* The third verse of *Bircas*

1. [The Aramaic version of the verses which appear in *Targum Onkelos* in all printed *Chumashim* today is a later addition, which was not in the *Targum* as it was originally handed down.]

כֹּהֲנִים

עַם קְדוֹשֶׁךָ — כָּאָמוּר:

Facing the Ark, the Kohanim raise their hands and begin pronouncing the prior blessing. Upon reaching וְצִוָּנוּ *they face the congregation and complete the blessing. The congregation, but not the chazzan, responds* אָמֵן.

בָּרוּךְ אַתָּה יהוה, אֱלֹהֵינוּ מֶלֶךְ הָעוֹלָם, אֲשֶׁר קִדְּשָׁנוּ בִּקְדֻשָּׁתוֹ שֶׁל אַהֲרֹן וְצִוָּנוּ לְבָרֵךְ אֶת עַמּוֹ יִשְׂרָאֵל בְּאַהֲבָה.

Kohanim — the blessing of peace — merges the material blessings of the first blessing with the spiritual beneficence of the second and braids them into a *three-ply cord not easily severed.*]

Alternatively, the tripartite nature of *Bircas Kohanim* corresponds to three classes of people: צַדִּיקִים, בֵּינוֹנִים, רְשָׁעִים, *righteous, average, wicked.* יְבָרֶכְךָ ה׳, *May HASHEM bless you,* is said to the righteous who are worthy of blessing. יָאֵר ה׳ פָּנָיו אֵלֶיךָ, *May HASHEM shine His face on you,* is for the average people, for although God always looks at people and their deeds, he does not necessarily do so with פָּנִים מְאִירוֹת, *a shining countenance.* The third verse, יִשָּׂא ה׳ פָּנָיו אֵלֶיךָ, *May HASHEM lift His face to you,* is the blessing given to the wicked, for God ordinarily would wish to avert his gaze from them (so to speak) and look at the ground to avoid seeing them (*Anaf Yosef* citing *Toldos Yitzchak*).

Dover Shalom offers another ex-

planation of the phrase *tripartite in the Torah.* In the Torah the blessing contains three verses, but there are times when the three are recited as one. The Mishnah (*Sotah* 7:6) teaches that in the Temple the three verses were recited as בְּרָכָה אַחַת, *a single blessing,* with no pause between verses for the *amen* response.

כֹּהֲנִים עַם קְדוֹשֶׁךָ — *Kohanim, Your holy people.*

This expression appears in the confessional prayers of the *Kohen Gadol* during the Yom Kippur service. The Mishnah (*Yoma* 4:2) records his words: 'I beg of You, HASHEM, I have acted wickedly ... I and my family, and the children of Aaron, עַם קְדוֹשֶׁךָ, Your holy people ...'. Reference to *Kohanim* as a holy people is based on the verse (*I Chronicles* 23:13): *And Aaron was set apart that he be sanctified holy of holies, he and his sons forever ... and to bless in My Name forever* (*Iyun Tefillah*).

אֲשֶׁר קִדְּשָׁנוּ — The Prior Blessing ﮠ

[See "The Kohen's Prior Blessing", p. 40]

The *Kohanim* may not begin their prior blessing until the *chazzan* has summoned them formally by reciting the word 'Kohanim' (*Shulchan Aruch* 128:18). [Where the congregation responds עַם קְדוֹשֶׁךָ כָּאָמוּר, the *Kohanim* must wait for the people to finish their declaration.]

Many authorities do not permit the *chazzan* to respond *amen* as it would constitute an interruption of his *Amidah.* If the *chazzan* reads from a *siddur* he may respond *amen* after each of the three verses of *Bircas Kohanim,* for this *amen* is considered a part of the prayer, not an interruption. However, if he calls out the words

Kohanim,

Your holy people — as it is said:

Facing the Ark, the Kohanim raise their hands and begin pronouncing the prior blessing. Upon reaching וְצִוָּנוּ they face the congregation and complete the blessing. The congregation, but not the chazzan, responds אָמֵן.

Blessed are You HASHEM, our God, King of the universe, Who has sanctified us with the holiness of Aaron and commanded us to bless His people Israel with love.

from memory then his responding *amen* may cause him to forget where he is up to and so he should not respond (*Mishnah Berurah* 128:71).

אֲשֶׁר קִדְּשָׁנוּ — *Who has sanctified us* [i.e. the *Kohanim*].

The blessing is worded to make clear that the holiness of Aaron was neither a usurpation on his part nor a show of nepotism by his brother, Moses, but was Divinely ordained. At the onset of the seven-day dedication of the מִשְׁכָּן, *Tabernacle*, God told Moses to sanctify Aaron and his sons in full view of the entire nation. *And he gathered the congregation at the entrance to the Tent of Meeting; and Moses said to the congregation, 'This is the matter which HASHEM has commanded to do'* (*Leviticus* 8:4-5). *Rashi* explains: [Moses said,] 'These things which I do before you, I have been commanded by the Holy One, Blessed is He, to do. Do not think that I do them for my own honor or for my brother's honor.'

On the eighth day Moses summoned Aaron and his sons, and the elders of Israel (ibid. 9:1). The Torah goes on to describe the service performed by the *Kohen Gadol* on Yom Kippur. It is understandable that the *sons* of Aaron should be called to be taught this service for one of them would eventually succeed his father as *Kohen Gadol*. But why were the elders invited — they could never perform this service? Again *Rashi* explains: He called the elders to teach them that Aaron's accession to the office of *Kohen Gadol* was Divinely or-

dained, lest they say that he usurped the position.

בְּקְדֻשָׁתוֹ שֶׁל אַהֲרֹן — *With the holiness of Aaron.*

Just as the selection of Israel as the Holy Nation is not dependent solely upon the deeds of each individual member, but on the holiness of their forebears — indeed, it is the very sanctity of the Patriarchs which embued their descendants with a capacity for holiness — so is the sanctity of the *Kehunah* [priesthood] unique among the descendants of Aaron. One who would endow *Kehunah* merely on the basis of personal deeds may be compared to Korach in his rebellion against Moses and Aaron.

Korach's specific mutiny was aimed at the appointment of Aaron as *Kohen Gadol*. 'The entire congregation, all of them, are holy ones and HASHEM is in their midst! Why do you [Moses and Aaron] exalt yourselves above the assembly of HASHEM?' (*Numbers* 16:3). Korach argued that *Kehunah* should be divorced from familial binds. But in so doing he undermined the foundation of the Holy Nation, because denial of the inborn sanctity of Aaron's offspring leads to a denial of the innate holiness of Israel's children. By Korach's logic, one could argue that God's selection of Israel as His people could be voided by the nation's sinfulness in the future.

Moses responded 'Morning [will come] and HASHEM will make known who is His and who is the holy one ...' (Numbers 16:5). Moses meant, 'Just as the Creator set boundaries between day and night and has *separated between the light and the darkness' (Genesis 1:4)*, and made this a necessary condition for the future of His world, in like fashion has He *'set you [Israel] apart from all the nations' (Leviticus 20:26)* to be His Holy Nation. And so has He set Aaron apart *that he be sanctified [as] holy of holies, he and his sons forever (I Chronicles 23:13).* Moses alluded to this when he said, *Morning [will come] and HASHEM will make known;* the coming of morning will demonstrate that God made inviolable boundaries in creation. Thus, concluded Moses, 'if you can tear down the barrier that God established between light and darkness and cause them to intermingle, only then can you also remove the separation with which He has sanctified Aaron above the Holy Nation' *(Bamidbar Rabbah* 18:7). This is the implication of the *Kohanim's* words when they praise *God Who sanctified us with the holiness of Aaron ...* *(Mei Meirom).*

Although the *Kohanim* have been *sanctified with the holiness of Aaron,* their level of holiness is not equal to his. This distinction is inferred from the wording of this blessing.

Both Hebrew and English have two forms to express possession: קְדֻשָׁתוֹ שֶׁל אַהֲרֹן, *the holiness of Aaron,* and the shorter form, קְדֻשַׁת אַהֲרֹן, *Aaron's holiness.* Although the two English forms are synonymous, the Talmud *(Shabbos* 29b) notes that there is a difference between the two Hebrew forms, when they are used with exactitude. In discussing wicks made by rolling pieces of cloth, the Talmud explains that פְּתִילָה שֶׁל בֶּגֶד means a *wick made from a piece of cloth* which had originally been part of a larger garment. The shorter פְּתִילַת הַבֶּגֶד describes *a wick rolled from a complete garment* (albeit a very small one). In the latter case the wick and the garment are identical, in that the entire garment is being used as a wick.

Applying this distinction to our blessing, had the Sages employed the term קְדֻשַׁת אַהֲרֹן, it would have meant that the holiness of *Kohanim* in all generations is identical to that of Aaron. But this is not so. Even those who succeeded Aaron as *Kohanim Gedolim* were not on the same plane of sanctity as the progenitor of the priestly family. [As an example, according to *Vilna Gaon,* Aaron was permitted to enter the Holy of Holies at will, provided that he performed a service similar to that described in chapter 16 of *Leviticus.* His successors, however, could perform this service and enter the Holy of Holies only on Yom Kippur.] An ordinary *Kohen* can certainly not consider his special measure of sanctity equal to that of Aaron. Thus the text of the blessing reads: בִּקְדֻשָּׁתוֹ שֶׁל אַהֲרֹן, implying that the *Kohanim* declare themselves to have but *a fraction of Aaron's holiness (Tzilusa DeAvraham* citing *Makor HaBerachah).*

בְּאַהֲבָה — *With love.*

I.e. the *Kohanim* are to feel love for the congregation when they pronounce the blessings.

Although all *mitzvos* should be performed with an outpouring of love for the Creator, only regarding *Bircas Kohanim* is this love mentioned in the blessing which precedes its performance. The addition of the phrase *with love* is based upon *Zohar (Naso* 147b): "Any *Kohen* who does not have love for the congregation or for whom the congregation has no love, may not raise his hands to bless the congregation — as we find: טוֹב־עַיִן הוּא יְבֹרָךְ, *He who has a good eye, he shall be blessed (Proverbs* 22:9). But the word is spelled deficiently — יְבֹרָךְ instead of יְבוֹרָךְ — a spelling that can be vocalized יְבָרֵךְ, *he shall bless.* Thus by omitting one letter Scripture implies another interpretation, namely: *Only he who has a good eye,* יְבָרֵךְ, *he shall bless" (Magen Avraham* 128:18).

Amudei Shamayim bases the inclusion of this phrase, *with love,* on a different verse: *Trustworthy are the bruises* — i.e., admonitions — *of one's* beloved, while the kisses — i.e., bless-ings — of an enemy are heavy (Proverbs 27:6). Thus we are told: worthless are the blessings of a Kohen who is the 'enemy' of the congregations he blesses.

According to an alternative in-terpretation, with love does not modify to bless but Who has ... commanded us .... Thus, it was with love for Israel that God commanded the Kohanim to bless His nation (R' Yehudah ben Yakar).

On his first day as Kohen Gadol, Aaron blessed Israel: Aaron raised his hands toward the nation and blessed them (Leviticus 9:22), but we are not told what he said (Ramban). This teaches that a person must rejoice in his

fellow Jew's good fortune until his heart becomes filled with love, joy and bless-ing — a blessing so great that mere words cannot express it. His blessing must be so overflowing with love that the very movements of his hands must express his joy and love .

Raising the hands is a symbol of a heart pouring forth blessing and joy from a treasure trove of happiness. Raising the hands is not a sterile act — it must be a wholehearted expression of the hope and blessing which are hidden in the soul. An ocean of inexpressible joy issues from a pure soul; and the purer the soul, the purer the blessing (Or Chadash).

◆§ דַּבֵּר אֶל אַהֲרֹן — Scripture's Introductory Verse

The three verses of Bircas Kohanim are prefaced in the Torah with וַיְדַבֵּר ה' אֶל־מֹשֶׁה לֵּאמֹר דַּבֵּר אֶל־אַהֲרֹן וְאֶל־בָּנָיו לֵאמֹר כֹּה תְבָרֲכוּ אֶת־בְּנֵי יִשְׂרָאֵל אָמוֹר לָהֶם, And HASHEM spoke to Moses saying, 'Speak to Aaron and his sons saying, "So shall you bless the Children of Israel saying to them ... "'(Numbers 6:22, 23).

דַּבֵּר אֶל אַהֲרֹן וְאֶל בָּנָיו — Speak to Aaron and his sons.

Since the Priestly Blessings can be given only by the Kohanim, God in-structed Moses to direct the command-ment exclusively to Aaron and his sons. None but they could participate in ex-tending these blessings to the Jewish people (Sifre).

This should not be construed to mean that the power to confer or withhold blessings is vested in the Kohanim — only God has the power to assure peo-ple of success, abundance, and hap-piness (see below). Rather the Kohanim are given the duty of pronouncing God's blessings, just as they are the only ones charged with the performance of the Temple service. The recitation of these blessings is part of their Temple duties, and it was after completing the sacrificial service that Bircas Kohanim was pronounced. In our daily prayer service, too, the chazzan recites Bircas Kohanim after the blessing [רְצֵה] beseeching God to return the Temple service of Jerusalem (R' Hirsch).

What is the purpose of having the Kohanim pronounce the words, when it is obvious that only God has the power

to bless? And what is meant by the verse following the three blessings: And they shall place My Name upon the Children of Israel, and I shall bless them — what is the meaning and purpose of 'placing God's Name'? And why does God say I shall bless them, in conjunc-tion with the Priestly Blessing?

The basis of our faith is that all good and bad, success and failure, whether they befall the community or the in-dividual, are not coincidence or the result of man's power, but the will of God. As agents of God, the Kohanim have the mission of teaching Israel this principle. Each of the Priestly Blessing's three parts stresses this: May HASHEM bless ... May HASHEM shine ... May HASHEM lift ... If the Kohanim are successful in their role, as teachers, they will have indelibly placed God's Name on Israel, by making the people aware of God's infinite power and unbounded presence. Then Israel will be worthy of blessing, and God can say, I shall bless them (Akeidah).

כֹּה תְבָרֲכוּ — So shall you bless.

This is the same blessing Aaron con-ferred upon the people when the Tabernacle was inaugurated. There (Leviticus 9:22), the Torah did not give us the text of Aaron's blessing; that was left for this chapter, which lists not only the text but God's command that the Kohanim recite the same formula forever (Rashi to Leviticus 9:22).

Ramban suggests that Aaron may have composed his own blessing at the inauguration, but here God, Himself, ordained the text that would be used for all time.

R' Hirsch notes that it is an essential part of Judaism that we are to perform the commandments ordained by God, not that we create our own version of religion. Accordingly, the Kohanim were clearly instructed so shall you bless. The blessings would be meaningful only if they were given as God willed. This principle was strikingly affirmed upon the occasion of a great national tragedy: Almost immediately after Aaron gave the initial Priestly Blessings (Leviticus 9:22), his two eldest sons, Nadav and Avihu, took it upon themselves to bring to the Tabernacle an offering that was not ordained by God. Rather than contenting themselves with being instruments of His will, they wished to innovate their own service — and they were killed by a miraculous flame for their temerity (Leviticus 10:1-2).

In Kabbalistic terms, the word כה, so, has the connotation of uncompromising finality. It is an expression of the attribute of מַלְכוּת, kingship [הַמִּדָה הָעֲשִׂירִית, the Tenth Attribute], which signifies the final step in bringing an idea into public fruition. For this reason, the prophets, who revealed God's will to the masses, commonly introduced their message with the words כה אָמַר ה׳, so said HASHEM. Thus, this opening word of the commandment indicates that God's desire to bless is to be carried out in the world. The blessing is pronounced by the Kohanim who represent חֶסֶד, kindness [for they are successors of Aaron, who is the epitome of אֹהֵב שָׁלוֹם וְרֹדֵף שָׁלוֹם, the lover of peaceful harmony and the pursuer of peaceful harmony (Avos 1:12)]. Thus the Kohanim take the concept of blessing from its birth — in God's desire to be kind to Israel — to its final expression on earth (R' Bachya).[1]

תְבָרְכוּ — Shall you bless.

Midrash Tanchuma (Nasso 8) relates that Israel complained to God that it wished to be blessed by Him directly, and does not require the blessings of Kohanim. God replied, 'Although I said to the Kohanim that they are to bless you, it is I Who stand with them and bless you.'[2]

1. Commentators find various allusions in the numerical value of כה, which is twenty-five. R' Bachya notes that the Torah gives twenty-four kinds of tithes and gifts to the Kohanim [כ״ד מַתְּנוֹת כְּהוּנָה]. To this the Torah now adds a twenty-fifth: the power to pronounce God's blessings upon Israel.

Baal HaTurim notes that the verse שְׁמַע יִשְׂרָאֵל, Hear O Israel, contains twenty-five letters. The Torah mentions twenty-five times that God blesses Israel, and it speaks of peace twenty-five times.

☙ ☙ ☙

A story is told about R' Akiva Kohen who passed away in 1496. R' Akiva, with his twelve sons and thirteen daughters, lived in Prague where he built a magnificent synagogue and study hall. One of his daughters, Yocheved, married R' Shabsai Horowitz who was a Levite. Their son R' Avraham was the father of the Sh'lah HaKadosh. R' Akiva's other twelve daughters all married Kohanim. When he ascended the duchan flanked by his twelve sons and twelve sons-in-law, R' Akiva would boast, 'I am truly fulfilling the verse כה תְבָרְכוּ, with כ״ה, i.e., twenty-five, shall you bless' (Taamei HaMinhagim, Kontres Acharon 117).

2. K'sav Sofer finds a homiletical meaning in Israel's strange choice of words: אֵין אָנוּ צְרִיכִין, we do not need [the blessings of Kohanim]. Human beings can bless only according to their own conception of good. The poor man dreams of wealth, the childless couple of children, the sick person of robust health. But it happens all too often that such 'blessings' bring sadness to their recipients. Man is often frustrated by his 'dreams come true'. Therefore, Israel says, 'We

In a similar vein, *Rashbam* and *Abarbanel* comment that the *Kohanim's* pronouncement is in the nature of one who prays that God fulfill his good wishes for a friend. There, too, the well-wisher knows full well that only God has the power to confer real, rather than verbal, blessings.

[In this light, and in line with the above-mentioned comments of *R' Hirsch*, the *Kohanim* are the agents to pronounce God's blessings just as they are the agents to perform His Temple service. Indeed, *Bircas Kohanim* is the only vestige of the Temple service remaining to us in exile, and it is because the blessings have such standing that they may not be pronounced in the prescribed manner by non-*Kohanim*. Or (see *R' Bachya* above), the *Kohanim* as the embodiment of חֶסֶד, *kindness*, are God's chosen vehicle to bless His people.]

The expression כֹּה תְבָרֲכוּ, *so shall you bless*, is a positive commandment; any *Kohen* who refuses to pronounce *Bircas Kohanim* is in violation of this precept (*Sotah* 38a).

Homiletically, the phrase can be understood differently. The benevolent *Kohanim* want nothing more than to bless Israel; they require no direct commandment to do so. All they need is to be told *how* to bless Israel. Therefore, the Torah does not explicitly command, it says only what the text of the blessing should be (*Imrei Emes*).

אָמוֹר לָהֶם — *Saying to them.*
It is not clear who is to say what to whom. There are three interpretations:

— The priests are told by Moses that they are to recite the following blessings to the listening congregation (*Rashi* according to *Mizrachi*).

— The people are commanded to say to *them* [the *Kohanim*] that they are to pronounce the blessing (*Onkelos; Sotah* 38a).

— The *chazzan* is to call out the blessings word by word to the *Kohanim*, who in turn are to repeat them in blessing the people (*Sifre* 39).

R' Hirsch gives a reason for the procedure that the *Kohanim* ascend to deliver the blessings only when called upon by the *chazzan*, and then repeat them word for word after him. This practice emphasizes that fact that the *Kohanim* have no power of their own, they are nothing more than the passive tools through which God blesses Israel. Therefore, the very ceremony is designed to dispel the impression that the *Kohanim* make independent decisions (*Horeb*).

⇜§ The Blessings

After the *Kohanim* have completed the prior blessing they may not begin *Bircas Kohanim* until every member of the congregation has completed his *amen* response, because each person must hear every word uttered by the *Kohanim*. Thus, even if some individuals — in their ignorance — draw out the *amen* longer than they should, the *Kohanim* must wait until they have finished. According to prevalent custom that the *chazzan* precedes the *Kohanim* in reading the words, it is the *chazzan* who must wait for the *amen* to be completed. Since his words are directed to the *Kohanim* and need not be heard by the congregation, it is sufficient that he wait for a majority of the assembled to finish. This same rule applies to the second and third verse; they should not be begun until the *amen* response is concluded (*Mishnah Berurah* 128:65).

Likewise the *Kohanim* may not recite any word until the *chazzan* has completed it; nor may the *chazzan* read a word before the *Kohanim* have finished the previous word. Additionally, the people must wait until the *Kohanim* have completed their pronouncement before responding with *amen* (*Shulchan Aruch* 128:18).

---

do not *need* blessings of whose outcome we can never be sure. Instead, we want only what God considers to be of benefit to us.'

The chazzan reads each word of Bircas Kohanim aloud and the Kohanim pronounce it after him. The congregation silently concentrates on their words. The secondary verses should not be said aloud but may be scanned by the eyes.

יְבָרֶכְךְ   יְבָרֶכְךָ יהוה מִצִּיוֹן, עֹשֵׂה שָׁמַיִם וָאָרֶץ.

יהוה   יהוה אֲדוֹנֵינוּ, מָה אַדִּיר שִׁמְךָ בְּכָל הָאָרֶץ.

◄§ יְבָרֶכְךְ — The First Blessing

יְבָרֶכְךָ ה׳ — May HASHEM bless you.

[As will be seen from Sifre and most of the commentaries that will be cited, the first blessing refers to material prosperity, the second to the spiritual blessings of Torah knowledge and inspiration, and the last blessing to God's compassion above and beyond what one deserves, as expressed in forgiveness of sin and the giving of peace.]

May God give you the many blessings that are specified in the Torah such as those mentioned in *Deuteronomy* (28:1-14): that Israel be triumphant over its enemies and superior to other nations, that its crops and business ventures succeed, its offspring and flocks be abundant and healthy, and so on (*Sifre*).[1]

May your possessions increase (*Rashi*), as well as your lifetimes (*Ibn Ezra*).

Though it is clear that in the Divine scheme and in Israel's aspirations such material benefits are secondary to spiritual success, nevertheless אִם אֵין קֶמַח אֵין תּוֹרָה, *if there is no flour there is*

---

1. Although the previous verse spoke in plural, all the blessings are in the singular. This alludes to the blessing without which all the others can become meaningless — Jewish unity (*R' Shlomo Leib of Lenchna*).

◄§ The Secondary Verses

In most *siddurim* a series of verses — which we shall call "secondary verses" — is printed alongside the fifteen words of *Bircas Kohanim*. In some *siddurim* two such series are found, one usually printed in smaller letters. The majority of early *siddurim* containing these verses have the series presented here, the one that is usually found in larger type. *Kol Bo* uses a different series, the one usually printed in smaller letters. Later printers combined both versions, distinguishing between them by using different size type.

The function of these secondary verses presents a difficulty already dealt with in the Talmud (*Sotah* 39b-40a). There the question is posed: At the time the *Kohanim* bless the people, what do they [the people] say? R' Zeira cites the teaching of R' Chisda that they should recite the three consecutive verses which each begins בָּרְכוּ ה׳, *Bless HASHEM* (Psalms 103:20-22). The *Gemara* continues with different sets of three verses to be recited at times other than the daily *Shacharis*. Thus, at the Sabbath *Mussaf* service, at the *Minchah* service of fast days, and at *Ne'ilah*, different verses are to be recited by the congregation. Each set consists of three verses corresponding to the three verses of *Bircas Kohanim*. [It is interesting to note that not one of the secondary verses found in our *siddurim* today is among those enumerated in the Talmud. Although the first one on our list is suggested, it is rejected.] Various opinions are then expressed regarding whether they are said between the verses pronounced by the *Kohanim* or while the *Kohanim* pronounce the Name of God; whether each of the three secondary verses is recited once or all three verses are repeated each time; and whether these verses are recited only at *Bircas Kohanim* in the Temple or even in the synagogue. Finally raised is the question of whether to say them at all. R' Chanina bar Papa opposes the practice and offers: Is it possible that a servant should receive a blessing and not listen to it! [That is to say, the servant should not speak while his master is blessing him.] R' Acha bar Chanina disagrees: Is it possible that a servant receives a blessing and not respond favorably to it [by praising his master]! Thus the function of the secondary verses is a show of gratitude to God for ordaining the blessing of the *Kohanim*.

In closing, the Talmud quotes R' Abahu: At first I would say these verses, but when I

The chazzan *reads each word of* Bircas Kohanim *aloud and the* Kohanim *pronounce it after him. The congregation silently concentrates on their words. The secondary verses should not be said aloud but may be scanned by the eyes.*

May [He] bless you

May HASHEM — Who makes heaven and earth — bless you from Zion.

HASHEM

HASHEM, our Lord, how mighty is Your Name throughout the earth!

no Torah (*Avos* 3:15). God blesses Israel with prosperity to enable the people to devote themselves to Torah study and fulfillment (*Sforno*).

R' Hirsch explains why *Sifre*, as followed by the above commentators, takes this blessing to involve material matters. Since this verse of the blessing concludes with a prayer that God 'protect' us, it is clear that we speak of benefits that require protection even after they have been granted. Spiritual blessings are 'protected' only by the personal worthiness of the recipients,

but material blessings are always subject to outside danger.

Haamek Davar notes that the term 'blessing' as used here is a general one; it does not clarify what sort of increase is meant. The exact form of the blessing must depend on the needs of each individual. The student will be blessed in his learning and the merchant in his business, just as someone's gratitude for God's blessing must be expressed according to the degree and form of the prosperity granted him (see *Deuteronomy* 16:17).

THE SECONDARY VERSES

noticed that R' Abba of Acco did not recite them, I, too, stopped this practice. Most halachic authorities favor this view. *Shulchan Aruch (Orach Chaim* 128:26) rules: 'While the *Kohanim* pronounce the blessing, [the congregation] should not recite any verses but should concentrate silently upon the blessing.'

To this, *Rama* adds: 'However, since nowadays the *Kohanim* draw out their tunes it has become customary to recite verses ... but it is better not to recite them.'

Most authorities agree that no verses should be recited at all. Some permit the verses to be read in an undertone while the *chazzan* calls out the words of the blessing. In any case, the practice of the masses who read these verses aloud — and especially of those who repeat the words of *Bircas Kohanim* after the *chazzan* — is wrong and has no halachic basis (*Mishnah Berurah* 128:103).

יְבָרֶכְךָ ה' מִצִּיּוֹן — *May HASHEM ... bless you from Zion.*

In *Psalms* [134:2] this verse is preceded by שְׂאוּ יְדֵכֶם קֹדֶשׁ, *raise your hands in holiness,* וּבָרְכוּ אֶת ה', *and bless HASHEM. Radak* (following *Targum*) interprets: Raise your hands, *Kohanim*, in the place of holiness [i.e., upon the *duchan*] and recite HASHEM's blessing, which begins יְבָרֶכְךָ ה', *May HASHEM bless you.* מִצִּיּוֹן, *From Zion,* will God's blessing spread to all of Israel. For He is the Creator of the heavens and will cause them to rain their bounty down on the nation.

ה' אֲדֹנֵינוּ — *HASHEM, our Lord ...*

Psalms 8:2 reads: *HASHEM, our Lord, how*

mighty is Your Name throughout the earth, for it were fit that You place Your majesty above the heavens. The concluding verse of that Psalm (*v.* 10) repeats the first stich which speaks of God's might on earth, but omits any mention of His majesty in heaven. The Talmud (*Shabbos* 88b) explains: Rabbi Joshua ben Levi taught that when Moses ascended to heaven, the ministering angels said to the Holy One, Blessed is He, 'Master of the universe, what business has one who is born of woman among us?'

'He has come to receive the Torah,' was the Divine answer.

'What!' said the angels to Him, 'Are You about to bestow upon frail man that

וְיִשְׁמְרֶךָ. שָׁמְרֵנִי, אֵל, כִּי חָסִיתִי בָךְ.

The Kohanim sing an extended chant before saying וְיִשְׁמְרֶךָ, and the congregation says the following supplication in an undertone. On the Sabbath this supplication is omitted. When the Kohanim conclude וְיִשְׁמְרֶךָ, the congregation and chazzan respond אָמֵן.

וְיִשְׁמְרֶךָ — *And protect you.*

May God protect your newly gained blessing of prosperity so that bandits cannot take it away from you. This is a blessing only God can guarantee. A king who sends a huge gift to his servant cannot guard it against every danger. If armed robbers take it away, what good would it have been to the recipient? *(Rashi).*[1]

First, the *Kohanim* give the blessing, and then they say it will be protected. This is meant to imply that God's protection will be in direct proportion to

the size and extent of the blessing *(Ohr HaChaim).*

Furthermore, God will assure that what seemed to be a blessing will not become a curse *(Ohr HaChaim).* The scholar can easily turn haughty and the rich man can turn greedy and power-mad. Therefore, in addition to protecting us against loss of His blessing, God is asked to prevent it from turning sour *(Ha'amek Davar).*[1]

By their very nature physical blessings are fragile, because neither health, business conditions, nor tangible assets

---

1. Certainly a human king can dispatch armed guards to protect his endowment against theft. However, this protection is additional to and distinct from the king's present. Whereas when God bestows wealth, the safeguarding of that wealth is included in the original blessing *(Chiddushei HaRim* citing R' Bunam of P'shis'cha; *Siach Sarfei Kodesh* 3:166).

1. [Among the locations listed in *Deuteronomy* 1:1 as sites where Israel sinned during its forty year sojourn in the wilderness is דִי זָהָב, *Di-zahav* (lit., *enough gold).* But no place with that name is known to exist; nor does any other reference to Di-zahav appear in Scripture. The Talmud explains that the name is both an allusion to, and a reason for, the Golden Calf.]

The Academy of R' Yannai taught: Moses proclaimed before the Holy One, Blessed is He, 'Master of the world, Israel was tempted to build the Golden Calf because of the abundance of silver and (זָהָב) gold which you have given the people — until they were forced to cry, '(דַּי) Enough!'' '

R' Yochanan compared this to a man who bathed his son, anointed him with fragrant oil, wined and dined him, placed a purse around his neck, and left him at the door of a brothel. How can the son prevent himself from sinning! ...

R' Yonasan taught that the Holy One, Blessed is He, acknowledged Moses' rationalization when He said *(Hosea* 2:10): *And silver which I presented her in abundance — and gold — they used for the Baal (Berachos* 32a).

THE SECONDARY VERSES

cherished treasure that was with You for nine hundred and seventy four generations before the world was created? *What is the frail human that You should remember him, and the son of mortal man that You should be mindful of him? HASHEM, our Master, how mighty is Your Name [already] throughout the earth. For it were fit that You place Your majesty above the heavens!' (Psalms* 8:5,2).

The Holy One, Blessed is He, then called upon Moses to refute their objection ...

Moses said to them: "Of what use can the Torah be to you? ... It is written, *'Remember the Sabbath and keep it holy' (Exodus* 20:8). Do you work that you need rest? Again it is written, *'Honor your father and mother' (Exodus* 20:12). Have you a father and mother? And also it is written, *'You shall not murder, you shall not commit adultery, you shall not steal' (Exodus* 20:13). Does jealousy exist among you? Does an evil impulse exist among you?"

The angels at once acknowledged that God

and protect you. *Protect me, O God, for in You have I taken refuge.*

The Kohanim sing an extended chant before saying וְיִשְׁמְרֶךָ, and the congregation says the following supplication in an undertone. On the Sabbath this supplication is omitted. When the Kohanim conclude וְיִשְׁמְרֶךָ, the congregation and chazzan respond אָמֵן.

---

are permanent and unchanging. Nor are the character and ambitions of a human being. Therefore, we seek the blessing of God's protection, so that once given, his blessing will not fade away (*Malbim*).[1]

May God *bless you* with wealth and *protect you* so that you use the money to perform *mitzvos (Bamidbar Rabbah).* For, as the Sages teach in many places, the best way for someone to preserve his wealth is to use it for charity and good deeds. That assures him God's continued blessing (*Yalkut Yehudah*).

◄§ חֲלוֹם חָלַמְתִּי — Supplication Regarding Dreams

[See "Supplication Regarding Dreams" p. 43.]

The supplication regarding dreams is recited while the *Kohanim* chant the final word of each verse (*Rama* 128:45). It has become customary, however, for the *Kohanim* not to pronounce the final word until the congregation finishes the supplication. In the interim the *Kohanim* sing an extended chant to allow the congregation time to say the prayer (*Be'ur Halachah*).

In most communities it has become customary to recite this supplication only after the first two verses. After the third verse, a different prayer is recited: יְהִי רָצוֹן, *May it be acceptable* [p. 82]. *Mishnah Berurah* (130:5), however, follows *Vilna Gaon* who retains the original custom of reciting this supplication all three times.

Siddur HaAdmor HaZaken (Lubavitch) records the *Chabad*-Lubavitch custom of dividing the supplication into three parts. None of it is said until the *Kohanim* reach the last three words of *Bircas Kohanim*. One part is said before each of the three words.

The part until 'the dreams of the righteous Joseph' is said prior to וְיָשֵׂם, *and He*

---

1. The two wishes — that we be blessed with success and that it be preserved — are inseparable. We want our prosperity to come from a source and in a manner that will please God, otherwise why should he wish to protect it for us? A father will be happy to advise and help a son who amasses a fortune through hard work and honest dealing, but he will not wish to be associated with the profits of banditry and sin. Similarly, the *Kohanim* wish Israel that its success come about through God's blessing — through means that meet with His approval. Only then can we legitimately ask Him to protect our possessions (*Chafetz Chaim*).

THE SECONDARY VERSES

was right in choosing to move His Torah from heaven to earth, therefore it is written (*Psalms* 8:10) 'HASHEM our Master, how mighty is Your Name throughout the earth,' and no longer is it written, 'For it were fit that You place Your majesty above the heavens.'

שָׁמְרֵנִי ... — *Protect me* ...

[This is a fragment of a verse which reads in full; *A michtam* [crown] *unto David. Protect me, O God, for in You have I taken*

refuge (Psalms 16:1). Since it is improper to recite an incomplete verse (see *Taanis* 27b) the inclusion of this partial verse may perhaps be taken as an indication that the verses are not meant to be recited aloud, but are meant only to be seen and contemplated. Some *siddurim* do in fact cite the entire verse.

Presumably the verse is meant here to remind the recipient of the blessing that, *Bircas Kohanim* notwithstanding, one must strive to be worthy of Divine protection. This is the meaning of *for in You have I taken refuge.*]

רִבּוֹנוֹ שֶׁל עוֹלָם, אֲנִי שֶׁלָּךְ וַחֲלוֹמוֹתַי שֶׁלָּךְ; חֲלוֹם
חָלַמְתִּי וְאֵינִי יוֹדֵעַ מַה הוּא. יְהִי רָצוֹן
מִלְּפָנֶיךָ, יהוה אֱלֹהַי וֵאלֹהֵי אֲבוֹתַי, שֶׁיִּהְיוּ כָּל חֲלוֹמוֹתַי עָלַי וְעַל
כָּל יִשְׂרָאֵל לְטוֹבָה, בֵּין שֶׁחָלַמְתִּי עַל עַצְמִי וּבֵין שֶׁחָלַמְתִּי עַל
אֲחֵרִים וּבֵין שֶׁחָלְמוּ אֲחֵרִים עָלַי; אִם טוֹבִים הֵם, חַזְּקֵם וְאַמְּצֵם,
וְיִתְקַיְּמוּ בִי וּבָהֶם כַּחֲלוֹמוֹתָיו שֶׁל יוֹסֵף הַצַּדִּיק; וְאִם צְרִיכִים
רְפוּאָה, רְפָאֵם כְּחִזְקִיָּהוּ מֶלֶךְ יְהוּדָה מֵחָלְיוֹ, וּכְמִרְיָם הַנְּבִיאָה

shall grant; 'But if they require healing ... through the hand of Elisha' before לָךְ, to you; and 'And just as You transformed ... goodness' is said before שָׁלוֹם, peace. The final three words are said in an undertone as the Kohanim pronounce שָׁלוֹם.

When the Kohanim ascend the duchan on the Sabbath this supplication is omitted (Magen Avraham 128:70).

R' Mendel Kargau instituted in Paris that this supplication be recited only while the chazzan recites שִׂים שָׁלוֹם. R' David Tzvi Hoffmann subsequently introduced this practice in Berlin (Melamed LeHo'il I, 113).

חֲלוֹם חָלַמְתִּי וְאֵינִי יוֹדֵעַ מַה הוּא — I have dreamed a dream but I do not know what it indicates.

In dreams one is able to soar above his body and attain the higher spiritual forces of eternal life.R' Yosef Karo (Maggid Meisharim) cites a teaching from his angelic instructor: During sleep the soul divests itself of the corporeal garb which inhibits its free movement during the day (VeAni Tefillah).

בֵּין שֶׁחָלַמְתִּי עַל עַצְמִי וּבֵין שֶׁחָלַמְתִּי עַל אֲחֵרִים — Those I have dreamed about myself, those I have dreamed about others.

First one prays for his own welfare, then for the welfare of others. This accords with the Talmudic dictum (Bava Metzia 62a) that when a life hangs in the balance, your life takes precedence over your colleague's life (Baruch She'amar).

Magen Avraham, however, maintains that the order should be reversed since, in situations where a life is not immediately at stake, one should pray for his fellow before praying for himself.

כַּחֲלוֹמוֹתָיו שֶׁל יוֹסֵף הַצַּדִּיק — Like the dreams of the righteous Joseph.

Joseph had dreams suggesting that he would dominate his brothers — dreams that caused his brothers to hate him (Genesis 37:5-11). It was not until twenty-two years later that his brothers finally bowed to him, without realizing he was Joseph (ibid. 42:6,9). Only then did Joseph know that his dreams had come true (Rashi).

וְאִם צְרִיכִים רְפוּאָה — But if they require healing.

Parallel to the phrase אִם טוֹבִים הֵם if they are good, we would expect to find וְאִם רָעִים הֵם, but if they are bad [or, evil], for many Scriptural passages describe רַע, bad [or evil], as the opposite of טוֹב, good (e.g., Deuteronomy 30:15; Isaiah 5:2; Ecclesiastes 12:14). But since God uses dreams as a medium of communication with man (see Numbers 12:6), and From the mouth of the Most High does not issue the evil along with the good (Lamentations 3:38), it is axiomatic that dreams are not incurably evil. The milder phrase וְאָם צְרִיכִים רְפוּאָה, if they require healing, is used, therefore, because of its implicit suggestion that even a terrible dream can be turned to good effect (Baruch She'amar).

כְּחִזְקִיָּהוּ מֶלֶךְ יְהוּדָה מֵחָלְיוֹ — Like Hezekiah, King of Judah, from his sickness.

II Kings (20:1-6) tells of King Hezekiah's mortal illness. The prophet

Master of the world, I am Yours and my dreams are Yours. I have dreamed a dream but I do not know what it indicates. May it be acceptable before You, HASHEM, my God and the God of my fathers, that all my dreams regarding myself and regarding all of Israel be good ones — those I have dreamed about myself, those I have dreamed about others, and those that others dreamed about me. If they are good, strengthen them, fortify them, make them endure in me and in them like the dreams of the righteous Joseph. But if they require healing, heal them like Hezekiah, King of Judah, from his sickness; like Miriam the prophetess from her tzaraas; like Naaman from his tzaraas; like the

Isaiah came and told him: 'Thus says HASHEM: Instruct your household — for you shall die, and you shall not live.'

Instead of losing hope for his life, Hezekiah turned his face to the wall and he prayed to HASHEM, saying, 'Accept my prayer, HASHEM. Remember now how I have walked before You with truthfulness and with wholeheartedness; that which is good in Your eyes have I done.' And Hezekiah wept — a great weeping.

'Return and say to Hezekiah, "Prince of my people, thus says HASHEM, God of your forebear David: I have heard your prayer; I have seen your tears. Behold! — I shall heal you. On the third day you shall ascend to the Temple of HASHEM. And I shall add to your days fifteen years ..." '(II Kings 20:1-6).[1]

וּכְמִרְיָם הַנְּבִיאָה מִצָּרַעְתָּה — (And) like Miriam the prophetess from her tzaraas.

When Miriam and Aaron learned that their brother Moses had refrained from family life with his wife from the time the Ten Commandments were given, they spoke disparagingly about him. Unknown to them, Moses had to do so because he had to remain in a state of purity at all times, since God could speak to him at any moment. For her unwarranted slander against Moses, Miriam was punished with tzaraas, a malady that left her only because Moses himself prayed for her recovery[2] (Numbers 12:1-15, see Rashi).

1. The Talmud interprets this encounter between the king and the prophet:

The Holy One, Blessed is He, brought suffering upon Hezekiah and ordered Isaiah to visit the sick king ... Isaiah visited him and said, 'Thus says HASHEM:Instruct your household — for you shall die [in this world,] and you shall not live [in the world to come].'

'Why will such great evil befall me?' asked the king.

The prophet replied, 'For you have not fulfilled the commandments be fruitful and multiply.' [Since you refused to bring life into the world, you shall be cut off from life — measure for measure.]

'But', Hezekiah explained, 'I have seen by the Divine Spirit that evil children will be born to me.'

To this Isaiah replied, 'Why do you involve yourself with the secrets of the All-Merciful? You must do as you are commanded — and that which is proper in the eyes of the Holy One, Blessed is He, He shall do'.

'If that is the case,' responded King Hezekiah, 'then give me your daughter in marriage. Perhaps our joint merits will allow virtuous offspring to issue from us.'

'But it is too late,' said Isaiah, 'the decree has already been handed down.'

'Son of Amotz, be done with your prophecy and take leave,' replied the king, 'for I have received a tradition from my forebear [i.e., David, (see II Samuel 24:16-17)]: even if a sharp sword lies on a person's neck, he should not restrain himself from seeking mercy' (Berachos 10a).

2. צָרַעַת, tzaraas, is an affliction mentioned in the Torah. The stricken person is known as a מְצֹרָע, metzora, (feminine, מְצֹרַעַת, metzoraas). The symptoms of the ailment are white spots on the skin (Leviticus 13:1-46). Although tzaraas is usually translated as leprosy, that disease

מִצָּרַעְתָּהּ, וּכְנַעֲמָן מִצָּרַעְתּוֹ, וּכְמֵי מָרָה עַל יְדֵי מֹשֶׁה רַבֵּינוּ, וּכְמֵי
יְרִיחוֹ עַל יְדֵי אֱלִישָׁע. וּכְשֵׁם שֶׁהָפַכְתָּ אֶת קִלְלַת בִּלְעָם הָרָשָׁע
מִקְּלָלָה לִבְרָכָה, כֵּן תַּהֲפֹךְ כָּל חֲלוֹמוֹתַי עָלַי וְעַל כָּל יִשְׂרָאֵל
לְטוֹבָה, וְתִשְׁמְרֵנִי וּתְחָנֵּנִי וְתִרְצֵנִי. אָמֵן.

וּכְנַעֲמָן מִצָּרַעְתּוֹ — (And) like Naaman from his tzaraas.

As commanding general of Aram's army, Naaman had won fame as a great warrior, but he was a metzora. Once, the Arameans captured a young Jewish girl, and gave her to Naaman's wife as a maid. The girl told her mistress that the prophet Elisha could cure Naaman. Naaman told the king of Aram what she said, and the king dispatched him to Eretz Yisrael with a letter to King Jehoram of Israel insisting that he cure Naaman. The Aramean king meant that the Israelite king should instruct the prophet Elisha to cure Naaman (Metzudos). But Jehoram refused to seek Elisha's intervention, for he had long ignored Elisha's admonitions to give up idol worship (Radak). Anguished and fearful, Jehoram rent his garments and said, 'Am I a god able to kill and resurrect that this is sent to me — to cure a man of his tzaraas. Therefore, know now and perceive that he seeks a pretext to attack me.'

But when Elisha heard what happened, he sent a message to the king: 'Why have you rent your garments? Let him come now to me, and he will know that there is a prophet in Israel.'

Naaman then came with his horses and chariot and stood at the door of Elisha's house. And Elisha sent him a messenger to say, 'Go and bathe seven times in the Jordan. Then your flesh shall be restored and you will be cleansed.'

Naaman was enraged at the 'insulting' suggestion that a mere bath in 'the waters of Israel' could cure him. Angrily, he turned to go back to Aram. But his servants pleaded with him, 'My sire, had the prophet spoken to you of a great task, would you not have fulfilled it? How much more when all he said to you is, "Bathe and be cleansed!"'

So Naaman followed Elisha's instructions and his flesh was restored as the flesh of a young lad, and he was cleansed (II Kings 5:1-14).

וּכְמֵי מָרָה עַל יְדֵי מֹשֶׁה רַבֵּינוּ — (And) like the waters of Marah through the hand of Moses our teacher.

After the splitting of the Sea of Reeds, the Israelites traveled for three days without finding water. Finally they found water in Marah, but it was bitter. The people complained to Moses, whereupon God showed him a piece of wood, which he tossed into the waters; and the waters were sweetened (Exodus 15:22-25).

does not have the symptoms described by Scripture. Moreover, the spontaneous cure mentioned in connection with tzaraas is unknown as a cure for leprosy.

From the case of the prophetess Miriam, who was stricken with tzaraas for speaking disparagingly about Moses, the Sages derive that this ailment is a punishment for לְשׁוֹן הָרַע, slander. The Torah exhorts us to remember what God did to Miriam and to beware of the plague of tzaraas (Deuteronomy 24:8,9).

In the wilderness, the desert habitation of Israel was divided into three camps, and the metzora was excluded from all three. In the center of the nation was the מִשְׁכָּן, Tabernacle, which was known as מַחֲנֵה שְׁכִינָה, the camp of the Shechinah [Divine Presence]. Surrounding the Tabernacle area was מַחֲנֵה לְוִיָה, the camp of the Levites. Surrounding the camp of the Levites was מַחֲנֵה יִשְׂרָאֵל, the camp of the Israelites, the area of the twelve tribes. Metzoraim were expelled from all three camps. This punishment is deserved by him, measure for measure. Since his foul tongue causes strife between friends and discord between husband and wife, he is paid in kind by being isolated from his friends and family, and even from other contaminated persons (see Rashi to Leviticus 13:46).

*waters of Marah through the hand of Moses our teacher; and like the
waters of Jericho through the hand of Elisha. And just as You transformed the curse of the wicked Balaam from a curse to a blessing, so
may You transform all of my dreams regarding myself and regarding
all of Israel for goodness. May You protect me, may You be gracious to
me, may You accept me. Amen.*

וּכְמֵי יְרִיחוֹ עַל יְדֵי אֱלִישָׁע — *And like the
waters of Jericho through the hand of
Elisha.*

The people of Jericho complained to
Elisha that the bad waters of their city
caused premature deaths. Elisha said,
'Bring me a new flask, and fill it with
salt.'

He threw the salt into the water, saying 'Thus says HASHEM: I have healed
these waters. From here there shall no
longer be death and untimeliness' (II
Kings 2:19-22).

Elisha's choice of salt as a cure for the
water is explained in *Likutei Torah* by
analyzing the functions of salt and
water in the Temple services. All offerings were salted before being placed in
the altar-pyre; and a water libation was
offered each day of the Succos festival.
Rashi (Leviticus 2:13) explains that God
made a covenant with the seas, that
their water would be used for libations
while their salt will be sprinkled on all
offerings. Thus the spiritual elevation
of the 'lower waters' is dependent upon
salt. This role of salt is inherent in its
Hebrew name מֶלַח which contains the
same letters as the root חלם, *to restore*
(see *Isaiah* 38:16 וְתַחֲלִימֵנִי, *restore me);*
thus Elisha used salt to 'restore' water to
health. [Perhaps there is further
significance in the use of this example
of healing in this prayer regarding
dreams. The root חלם, *to restore,* is also
the root of חֲלוֹם, *a dream.*][1]

וּכְשֵׁם שֶׁהָפַכְתָּ אֶת קִלְלַת בִּלְעָם הָרָשָׁע
מִקְּלָלָה לִבְרָכָה — *And just as You transformed the curse of the wicked Balaam
from a curse to a blessing.*

Although Balaam blessed the
Israelites three times, his true intention
was to curse them. Only through
Divine intercession were his words
reversed, as the Torah states: *For
HASHEM, your God, was unwilling to
listen to Balaam. So HASHEM, your
God, transformed — for your sake — the
curse into a blessing, for HASHEM, your
God, loves you (Deuteronomy 23:6).*

וְתִשְׁמְרֵנִי וּתְחָנֵּנִי וְתִרְצֵנִי — *(And) may You
protect me, (and) may You be gracious
to me, (and) may You accept me.*

Originally, the same supplication was
recited after each of the three verses,
only the last word was changed. After
the first verse which ends with וְיִשְׁמְרֶךָ,
may He watch over you, the supplication would end with וְתִשְׁמְרֵנִי, *may He
watch over me;* after the second, וּתְחָנֵּנִי,
may You favor me, corresponding to
וִיחֻנֶּךָּ, *may He favor you;* and וְתִרְצֵנִי,
may You accept me, follows the third
verse which ends in שָׁלוֹם, *peace,* for
peace can only come with acceptance of
one another *(Yerias Shlomo).* [Probably,
when it became customary to recite the
יְהִי רָצוֹן supplication after the third
verse, all three expressions were incorporated into this prayer and said after
each of the first two verses.]

1. *Baruch She'amar* wonders why the events mentioned in this supplication are not
enumerated in chronological order. [The difficulty is aggravated by the fact that our present-
day text is a corruption of the Talmudic version which lists only three incidents, the waters of
Marah, Miriam and King Hezekiah, and they *are* recorded in the sequence in which they occurred.]

Dover Shalom explains that sickness may take either of two forms: A change in one's
nature or physical being or an anomaly occurring at birth or earlier, where the essential being
is unchanged from its original state. Our supplication begins with three examples of sickness
that caused a change in one's physical condition: Hezekiah's illness, and Miriam's and
Naaman's *tzaraas.* Then came two incidents of sickness inherent from initial creation: the un-

יָאֵר אֱלֹהִים יְחָנֵּנוּ וִיבָרְכֵנוּ; יָאֵר פָּנָיו אִתָּנוּ, סֶלָה.

יהוה יְהֹוָה יְהֹוָה, אֵל רַחוּם וְחַנּוּן, אֶרֶךְ אַפַּיִם וְרַב חֶסֶד וֶאֱמֶת.

פָּנָיו פְּנֵה אֵלַי וְחָנֵּנִי, כִּי יָחִיד וְעָנִי אָנִי.

◄§ יָאֵר — The Second Blessing

יָאֵר ה' — *May HASHEM shine.*

This refers to מְאוֹר תּוֹרָה, *the light of Torah,* as we find *(Proverbs 6:23) For the commandment is a lamp and the Torah is a light (Sifre).*[1] [This is a blessing of spiritual growth, that our

lives be illuminated by the wisdom of the Torah and, as *Sifre* also says, the lights of the שְׁכִינָה, *God's Presence.* Having been blessed with material success and the essential wish that we use it for constructive ends as God has commanded us (see commentary to the

drinkable waters of Marah and Jericho. [This interpretation follows the view of R' Elazar (in *Mechilta*). But R' Yehoshua maintains that the waters had always been sweet but were made bitter temporarily in order to test Israel.] The ordering of these latter two follows the proper chronological sequence. The first three, however, are not in such order.

Dover Shalom continues. Cure may be effected in three ways: לְמַעֲלָה מִן הַטֶּבַע, *supernaturally,* with no human involvement; עַל פִּי תְּפִלָּה, *through prayer,* i.e., supernaturally but with human intervention; and, עַל פִּי הַטֶּבַע, *through natural means.* This is the sequence of our supplication: Hezekiah's cure came without human intercession [except for his own prayer]; Miriam was healed as a result of Moses' prayer; and Naaman was relieved of *tzaraas* by immersion in the river.

[Alternatively, cure may be effected either in an entirely supernatural manner through prayer or in a seemingly natural way through medication. The choice of curative procedure is dictated by the type of sin that was the underlying cause of the malady.

When the original iniquity was strictly בֵּין אָדָם לַמָּקוֹם, *between man and the Omnipresent,* as was King Hezekiah's refusal to bear children, the sinner's own repentance and prayer suffice to bring about forgiveness and healing. But when a sin בֵּין אָדָם לַחֲבֵרוֹ, *between man and his fellow,* is involved, then even 'the atonement service of Yom Kippur does not provide atonement until he appeases his fellow' *(Yoma 8:9).* Thus, Miriam's *tzaraas,* which she contracted as a result of her slanderous talk against Moses, could not be relieved until Moses' accepted her apology, something that he proved by praying for her.

In Naaman's case, Scripture records no sin to account for his *tzaraas.* According to *Rashi's* comment *(II Kings 5:1)* the entire incident is related only as an indication of miraculous deeds performed by Elisha. Thus, Naaman's cure had to come through an action demonstrating his faith in the prophet's words, even if this faith came only after he initially rebuffed Elisha's instructions.]

1. R' Yisrael Baal Shem Tov cited in *Kedushas Levi* to Exodus 15:1 explains the verse *(Psalms 121:5):* ה' צִלְּךָ, *HASHEM is your shade.* The usual interpretation of this verse is a metaphor for the Divine protection (shade) given the righteous against troubles, symbolized by the blazing sun. But on another plane, the words ה' צִלְּךָ may be translated *H ASHEM is your shadow.* When you jump, your shadow jumps; when you stand still, your shadow does too. Similarly, when Jews sway in prayer in the synagogue and cry out ... יְהֵא שְׁמֵיהּ רַבָּא, *May His great Name be blessed* ... God nods His head (so to speak) and says, 'Happy is the King who is praised thus in His own house' (cf. *Berachos* 3a). When the *Kohanim* bless the nation what does God do? He stands behind them, like a shadow, peering over their shoulders through their fingers (cf. Midrash cited on p. 32).

[But do not think that God will always be your "shadow". Only when you perform *mitzvos* and worthy deeds will He be beside you, following your every motion. But where there is no light, there is also no shadow — and the source of spiritual light is *the mitzvah* which *is a lamp* and *the Torah* which *is a light.*]

May [He] shine

HASHEM

His face

May God favor us and bless us; may He shine His face with us, Selah.

HASHEM, HASHEM, God, Merciful and Compassionate, Slow to Anger, and Abundant in Kindness and Truth.

Turn Your face to me and be gracious to me, for I am alone and I am afflicted.

previous blessing), we are prepared to accept the even greater blessing of receiving God's wisdom. For the performance of commandments refines and elevates a person so that he can become a receptacle for the Torah just as a *lamp* is a receptacle for light. Having blessed us with properly utilized prosperity, the *Kohanim* now bless us with spiritual growth.]

May God enlighten you so that you will be capable of perceiving the wondrous wisdom of the Torah and of God's intricate creation. Having received the blessing of prosperity, we have the peace of mind to go beyond the elementary requirements of survival (*Sforno*).

May God grant you children who will be Torah scholars (*Tanchuma*).

פָּנָיו — *His face.*

The term פָּנָיו, [*God's*] *face*, must be understood in a figurative sense since God is incorporeal and physical description cannot apply to him literally. In this context the human designation refers to God's revealed purpose in His rule of the universe [in the sense that someone's attitudes are apparent from the expression on his face] (*R' Hirsch; Ha'amek Davar*).

Through the teachings of the Torah and the prophets, God sheds light — יָאֵר, to shed אוֹר, *light* — upon His workings of the universe. Thus, we can perceive a purpose in creation that, in turn, helps us better to understand the greatness and will of the Creator (*R' Hirsch*). When this happens, all will understand that the material benefits of the first blessing came from Him, rather than by chance or natural causes (*Ha'amek Davar*).

THE SECONDARY VERSES

אֱלֹהִים יְחָנֵּנוּ — *May God favor us ...*

[The connection of this verse (*Psalms* 67:2) to the second verse of *Bircas Kohanim* is due to the obvious parallelism of the verses.]

יְחָנֵּנוּ ... וִיחֶנְךָ

וִיבָרְכֵנוּ ... יְבָרֶכְךָ

יָאֵר פָּנָיו ... יָאֵר ה' פָּנָיו

ה' ה' — *HASHEM, HASHEM ...*

[Here is another case of a partial verse (*Exodus* 34:6) being cited. See above s.v. שָׁמְרֵנִי.]

The Thirteen Attributes of Divine Mercy are enumerated in this verse and the one that follows it in the Torah: *Preserver of Kindness for thousands of generations, Forgiver of Iniquity, Transgression and Sin; He Who Erases ...* (*Exodus* 34:7). [A fuller treatment of the Thirteen Attributes appears in ArtScroll *Tashlich*, pp. 16-22.]

Sforno explains the seemingly redundant appearance of *HASHEM, HASHEM* in this verse. Firstly, *HASHEM* is the Creator Who brought every part of the universe into being. Additionally, *HASHEM* is the Preserver of the universe, continuously breathing new life into His world. [Perhaps the verse is appended here to remind the recipients of the blessing that the *Kohanim* are only conduits through which the flow of blessing descends from Above. The ultimate source of the blessings, however, is the Creator and Controller of the universe — וַאֲנִי אֲבָרֲכֵם, *and I shall bless them* (*Numbers* 6:27; see "Scripture's Concluding Verse", p. 84).]

פְּנֵה אֵלַי — *Turn Your face to me ...*

[The Psalmist (25:16) pleads for the same measure of Divine blessing and guidance invoked by the second verse of *Bircas Kohanim*.]

אֵלֶיךָ יהוה נַפְשִׁי אֶשָּׂא. **אֵלֶיךָ**

וִיחֻנֶּךָּ. הִנֵּה כְעֵינֵי עֲבָדִים אֶל יַד אֲדוֹנֵיהֶם, כְּעֵינֵי שִׁפְחָה אֶל יַד גְּבִרְתָּהּ, כֵּן עֵינֵינוּ אֶל יהוה אֱלֹהֵינוּ עַד שֶׁיְּחָנֵּנוּ.

The Kohanim sing an extended chant and the congregation says the following supplication in an undertone as after וִישְׁמְרֶךָ. *See above p.68.*

רִבּוֹנוֹ שֶׁל עוֹלָם, אֲנִי שֶׁלָּךְ וַחֲלוֹמוֹתַי שֶׁלָּךְ; חֲלוֹם חָלַמְתִּי וְאֵינִי יוֹדֵעַ מַה הוּא. יְהִי רָצוֹן מִלְּפָנֶיךָ, יהוה אֱלֹהַי וֵאלֹהֵי אֲבוֹתַי, שֶׁיִּהְיוּ כָּל חֲלוֹמוֹתַי עָלַי וְעַל כָּל יִשְׂרָאֵל לְטוֹבָה, בֵּין שֶׁחָלַמְתִּי עַל עַצְמִי וּבֵין שֶׁחָלַמְתִּי עַל אֲחֵרִים וּבֵין שֶׁחָלְמוּ אֲחֵרִים עָלַי; אִם טוֹבִים הֵם, חַזְּקֵם וְאַמְּצֵם, וְיִתְקַיְּמוּ בִי וּבָהֶם כַּחֲלוֹמוֹתָיו שֶׁל יוֹסֵף הַצַּדִּיק; וְאִם צְרִיכִים רְפוּאָה, רְפָאֵם כְּחִזְקִיָּהוּ מֶלֶךְ יְהוּדָה מֵחָלְיוֹ, וּכְמִרְיָם הַנְּבִיאָה מִצָּרַעְתָּהּ, וּכְנַעֲמָן מִצָּרַעְתּוֹ, וּכְמֵי מָרָה עַל יְדֵי מֹשֶׁה רַבֵּינוּ, וּכְמֵי יְרִיחוֹ עַל יְדֵי אֱלִישָׁע. וּכְשֵׁם שֶׁהָפַכְתָּ אֶת קִלְלַת בִּלְעָם הָרָשָׁע מִקְּלָלָה לִבְרָכָה, כֵּן תַּהֲפֹךְ כָּל חֲלוֹמוֹתַי עָלַי וְעַל כָּל יִשְׂרָאֵל לְטוֹבָה, וְתִשְׁמְרֵנִי וּתְחָנֵּנִי וְתִרְצֵנִי. אָמֵן.

יִשָּׂא יִשָּׂא בְרָכָה מֵאֵת יהוה, וּצְדָקָה מֵאֱלֹהֵי יִשְׁעוֹ. וּמְצָא חֵן וְשֵׂכֶל טוֹב בְּעֵינֵי אֱלֹהִים וְאָדָם.

וִיחֻנֶּךָ — *And be gracious to you.*
May He cause you to find חֵן, *favor* [in the eyes of others] *(Sifre)*. But if God has given us the benefits of the light of this Torah and of His Presence, what more 'favor' can be needed? A person can have a host of personal attributes, but unless his fellows appreciate and understand him, the relationship between them will not be good. The 'grace' that a person has is the quality of being liked by others. With this blessing, the *Kohanim* pray that after giving Israel material and spiritual success, God will enable the other nations to evaluate us properly *(Ohr HaChaim* according to *Degel Machneh Ephraim)*.

Ramban, however, interprets that Israel will find favor in God's eyes.

Sifre interprets: *God be gracious to you* by granting you Torah knowledge, as well as the wisdom and understanding to utilize it properly and fully. Accordingly, this term complements the first part of this blessing. May God grant you the Torah knowledge and insight to comprehend His purpose *(R' Hirsch)*.

Tanchuma homiletically derives the word from חֲנָיָה, *encamping* or *settling;* i.e., **May God's Presence be with you.**

[The term חֵן, *favor*, is used to indicate the bestowal of an undeserved gift (see *Rashi, Deuteronomy* 3:23). Thus, we are given the blessing that we may receive God's kindness even if it is unearned.

The *Chafetz Chaim* would pray: Master of the universe, even if we do not deserve your kindness, at least treat us according to Your attribute of giving undeserved gifts to Israel.]

◆§ יִשָּׂא — **The Third Blessing**

יִשָּׂא ה' פָּנָיו אֵלֶיךָ — *May HASHEM lift His face to you.*

'He will suppress His anger' *(Rashi)*.

upon you *To You, HASHEM, I uplift my soul.*

and be *Behold! As the eyes of servants to the hand of*
gracious *their masters, as the eyes of a maidservant to the*
to you. *hand of her mistress, so are our eyes to You,*
HASHEM our God, until He find favor with us.

The Kohanim sing an extended chant and the congregation says the following
supplication in an undertone as after וְיִשְׁמְרֶךָ. *See above p. 68.*

Master of the world, I am Yours and my dreams are Yours. I have
dreamed a dream but I do not know what it indicates. May it be acceptable before You, HASHEM, my God and the God of my fathers,
that all my dreams regarding myself and regarding all of Israel be good
ones — those I have dreamed about myself, those I have dreamed about
others, and those that others dreamed about me. If they are good,
strengthen them, fortify them, make them endure in me and in them
like the dreams of the righteous Joseph. But if they require healing,
heal them like Hezekiah, King of Judah, from his sickness; like Miriam
the prophetess from her tzaraas; like Naaman from his tzaraas; like the
waters of Marah through the hand of Moses our teacher; and like the
waters of Jericho through the hand of Elisha. And just as You transformed the curse of the wicked Balaam from a curse to a blessing, so
may You transform all of my dreams regarding myself and regarding
all of Israel for goodness. May You protect me, may You be gracious to
me, may You accept me. Amen.

May [He] *May he receive a blessing from HASHEM, and*
just kindness from the God of his salvation. And
lift *he will find favor and understanding in the eyes*
of God and man.

THE SECONDARY VERSES

אֵלֶיךָ ה׳ — *To You, HASHEM ...*
[This is a truncated verse which begins, *To
David ... (Psalms 25:1)*; see above, s.v.
שָׁמְרֵנִי.]
According to *R' Hirsch,* 'uplifting of one's
soul' symbolizes dutiful loyalty to God,
directing all of one's energies to become near
to Him. [Thus King David's declaration is an
apt companion to this verse which alludes to
spiritual blessings (see *Commentary*).]

הִנֵּה כְעֵינֵי — *Behold! As the eyes ...*
In discussing the function of these secondary verses (see above), we cited the two
Talmudic opinions regarding whether or not
they should be recited. In each view the congregation is compared to a servant receiving
a blessing from his master. Additionally *Sifre*
adduces this verse *(Psalms 123:2)* to show
that וִיחֻנֶּךָ is a request for God's largesse, un-

deserved though it may be. [This is similar to
a servant whose master has no obligation to
reward him, but does so out of his own
graciousness.]

יִשָּׂא ... וּמָצָא חֵן — *May he receive* [lit. *carry or
bear*] ... *And he will find favor ...*
[Of all the secondary verses, only here
have two distinct verses, indeed from two
different books of Scripture *(Psalms 24:5
and Proverbs 3:4)*, been appended. Interest-
ingly, these same two verses, in paraphrase,
are juxtaposed in *Bircas HaMazon,* where the
first-person singular has been changed to
first-person plural; *May we receive ... our
salvation. And may we find favor ...*]

After describing one whose hands are
clean, whose heart is pure and who restrains
his mind and mouth from evil thoughts and
falsehood, the Psalmist declares: *May he*

יְהוָה, חָנֵּנוּ, לְךָ קִוִּינוּ. הֱיֵה זְרֹעָם לַבְּקָרִים, אַף
יְשׁוּעָתֵנוּ בְּעֵת צָרָה.

אַל תַּסְתֵּר פָּנֶיךָ מִמֶּנִּי בְּיוֹם צַר לִי; הַטֵּה אֵלַי
אָזְנֶךָ; בְּיוֹם אֶקְרָא מַהֵר עֲנֵנִי.

אֵלֶיךָ נָשָׂאתִי אֶת עֵינַי, הַיֹּשְׁבִי בַּשָּׁמָיִם.

יְהוָה

פָּנָיו

אֵלֶיךָ

meaning that even if you are sinful God will show you special consideration and not punish you.

One's face is an indication of his attitude toward someone else. If one is angry at his neighbor, he refuses to look at him; and if one has wronged or is indebted to his neighbor, he is ashamed to face him. Therefore, when God turns His 'face' to Israel, so to speak, He symbolizes that He is not angry with us. As a result, we can lift our heads, despite our own unworthiness (Maharzu).

In varying forms, the Sages raise the question, how can it be said of God that He shows Israel special consideration that it does not deserve? Does not Scripture say of God (Deuteronomy 10:17) אֲשֶׁר לֹא יִשָּׂא פָנִים וְלֹא יִקַּח שֹׁחַד, Who does not lift a face [i.e., forgive undeservedly] and does not accept bribery?

Bloria the proselytess asked this question of Rabban Gamliel and an answer was given her by R' Yose the Kohen. He explained that God mercifully forgives sins committed against Him, but He refuses to show favor to those who sin against their fellow men unless they first placate and obtain forgiveness from the victim (Rosh Hashanah 17b).

Tosafos (ibid s.v. אשר) offers a different solution based on the contexts of the conflicting verses. Bircas Kohanim speaks of God's own behavior in that He lifts His face to sinners; He is consistently merciful and compassionate, willing to overlook and forgive transgressions. But the chapter in Deuteronomy says that God will not single out people for special treatment on the basis of their wealth, status, or lineage. The only distinguishing factor between individual Jews is merit.

The Midrash (Bamidbar Rabbah 11:4) notes the same contradiction but answers that Israel has earned God's special treatment. God says:

'Just as they are partial to me, so I am partial to them. How so? I have written in My Torah (Deut. 8:10), When you eat and are satisfied [i.e., when you have

---

THE SECONDARY VERSES

receive [or: He shall receive] a blessing from HASHEM...

[This leads to a question regarding the efficacy of Bircas Kohanim.] The righteous are promised material and spiritual blessings (see Leviticus 26:3-13 and Deuteronomy 28:1-14) regardless of the Kohanim, while the wicked are warned that Divine retribution will overtake them (see Leviticus 26:14-41 and Deuteronomy 28:15-68), despite Bircas Kohanim. To whom, then, does the blessing apply? R' Chaim Paltiel explains that the priestly blessing is reserved for the righteous and the good. Its purpose is to counter and negate any curses that may be hurled against them by vile persons such as Balaam, whom Heaven has granted the power of cursing. Additionally, Bircas Kohanim is efficacious

in hastening the fulfillment of the bounty promised to the righteous.

ה' חָנֵּנוּ — HASHEM, find favor with us ...
The Midrash (Bereishis Rabbah 98:14) teaches that all worthwhile things can be attained through hope and faith in God. Among those items enumerated are: Sanctification of God's Name, merit of the Patriarchs, the World to Come, forgiveness, and favor. Regarding the latter, the Midrash cites, HASHEM, find favor with us, for to You we have hoped ... (Isaiah 33:2).

אַל תַּסְתֵּר — Do not hide ...
The Kohanim beseech God to raise His countenance toward Israel; King David adds (Psalms 102:3), 'Even if You do not turn Your face to them, at least lean Your ear

Order of Bircas Kohanim   [78]

HASHEM, find favor with us, for You have we hoped! Be their power in the mornings, and our salvation in times of distress.

Do not hide Your countenance from me in a day that is distressing to me; lean Your ear toward me; in the day that I call, speedily answer me.

To You I raise my eyes, You Who sit in the Heavens.

eaten your fill] *you are to bless* [i.e., recite Grace after Meals to thank God for giving sustenance]. But a Jewish man sits with his children and family and they *lack* enough [food] to satisfy themselves — nevertheless they show me consideration and bless Me! They are strict with themselves [to bless] even for only the volume of an olive or an egg.' Therefore, *HASHEM will lift His face.*[1]

Malbim comments that God shows this special compassion because man's soul — his spiritual potential — can too easily be overwhelmed by the animal instincts of the body, which is its host.

R' Hirsch comments that the term God's *face* implies a high degree of spiritual intimacy. The climax of the material and intellectual blessings of previous verses are attained only when we realize that our greatest accomplishment is to serve God for no other purpose than to be worthy of His nearness.

1. *R' Bunam* of P'shis'cha explains that a gift may be so small as to be insignificant, but if the gift comes from the king, it will be treasured because of the majesty of the giver. Similarly, a small bit of food that leaves the eater hungry is hardly worthy of profuse thanks — but since Israel recognizes that all food is a gift of God, it thanks Him even for small amounts. That Israel has this degree of sensitivity proves that it is a superior people; and is therefore richly deserving of God's favorable treatment.

R' Chaim of Volozhin notes homiletically that Jewish greatness is demonstrated by a simple fact: when it comes to thanking God for nourishment, The Torah says *and you are satisfied*, yet Israel blesses Him for even a morsel. But when the Torah charges Israel to feed the poor until *they are satisfied* (Deuteronomy 26:12), Jews give until the hungry poor are truly satisfied — in the literal sense.

THE SECONDARY VERSES

towards them and answer their calls' (based on *Ibn Ezra*).

[Alternatively: Do not hide Your countenance by delaying the fulfillment of the blessings foretold in *Leviticus* (26:1-13) and *Deuteronomy* (28:1-14). Rather, *speedily answer me.* (See Commentary of *R' Chaim Paltiel* cited above s.v., יִשָּׂא בְרָכָה).]

אֵלֶיךָ נָשָׂאתִי — *To You I raise ...*

[This verse (*Psalms* 123:1) begins with the words, *A song of degrees ...* which are omitted here. See Commentary above, s.v., שָׁמְרֵנִי]

[The Talmud (*Rosh Hashanah* 17b) cites contradictary verses. In *Deuteronomy* (10:17) Moses describes God with the words ... *The Great, the Powerful, the Awesome, He Who does not raise a face, or accept* bribery. Yet in *Bircas Kohanim*, He is asked to *raise His Countenance* upon Israel. (For the Talmud's reconciliation of these verses see above.) *Tosafos* comments that according to the simple meaning of the verse (פְּשָׁט), *He does not raise a face* refers to God not elevating *man's* face in recognition of his wealth or privilege. Yet the Talmud renders the verse as if it applied to God's face. Perhaps the Talmud alludes here to a two-way action. God raises His face to man if man raises his face to God. Thus, *He does not raise a face* refers to both His face (so to speak) and man's. If this premise is true, then the second verse appended here, *to You I raise my eyes*, reminds the Jew that fulfillment of the *Kohen's* blessing is to some degree dependent upon his own relationship to God, and how he looks to Him.]

וְשָׂמוּ אֶת שְׁמִי עַל בְּנֵי יִשְׂרָאֵל, וַאֲנִי אֲבָרֲכֵם.

לְךָ יהוה, הַגְּדֻלָה וְהַגְּבוּרָה וְהַתִּפְאֶרֶת וְהַנֵּצַח
וְהַהוֹד, כִּי כֹל בַּשָּׁמַיִם וּבָאָרֶץ; לְךָ יהוה,
הַמַּמְלָכָה וְהַמִּתְנַשֵּׂא לְכֹל לְרֹאשׁ.

שָׁלוֹם שָׁלוֹם לָרָחוֹק וְלַקָּרוֹב, אָמַר יהוה,
וּרְפָאתִיו.

וְיָשֵׂם
לְךָ
שָׁלוֹם.

וַאֲנִי קִרֲבַת אֱלֹהִים לִי טוֹב, *But as for me,
the nearness of God is my goodness*
(Psalms 78:28).

God will not ignore your needs in
whatever direction they may be *(Ibn
Ezra)*, and He will save you from illness
and deprivation *(R' Bachya)*.

Sforno interprets this as the blessing
of the World to Come.

וְיָשֵׂם לְךָ שָׁלוֹם — *And may He grant you
peace.*

One may have prosperity, health,
food, and drink — but if there is no
peace it is all worthless. Therefore the
blessings are sealed with the gift of
peace *(Sifra, Bechukosei)*.

As the Sages taught in the very last
words of the Mishnah: R' Shimon ben
Chalafta said, 'The Holy One, Blessed is
He, could find no container that would
hold Israel's blessings as well as peace,
as it says *(Psalms 29:11), HASHEM will
give might to His nation, HASHEM will
bless His nation with peace (Uktzin
3:12).*

Sforno defines peace as spiritual eternity and perfection, unblemished by
punishment and failure to fulfill one's
potential (see *Sforno* here and to *Bereishis 49:15*).

The Midrash says, 'Peace when you
enter, peace when you leave, and
peaceful relations with everyone.' This

THE SECONDARY VERSES

וְשָׂמוּ אֶת שְׁמִי — *And they shall place My
Name ...*
I shall bless them refers to both the congregation and the *Kohanim* (see "Names of
the Blessing", p. 28).

לְךָ ה׳ — *To You, HASHEM ...*
This verse *(II Chronicles 29:11)* alludes to
many of the *Sefirah*-emanations (see below)
through which God's manifestations can be
perceived by man. *Zohar* (III, 146b) teaches
that the ten fingers of the *Kohen's* uplifted
hands represent the ten *Sefiros*, each of
which is invoked by *Bircas Kohanim.*
Man can have no conception of God
Himself, for His true Being is beyond human
intelligence. All we can know are His
manifestations such as mercy, power, judgment, and so on. Given the fact that we cannot perceive God directly, these manifestations can come to us only through intermediaries. These intermediaries are called
Sefiros, generally translated *emanations.*

In the terminology of the *Sefiros*, כֶּתֶר,
Crown, is above all the other emanations
and, like a crown that rests above the head
and encompasses it, the כֶּתֶר, *Crown*, is not
only higher than the others, but includes
them all. It is the 'bridge' between God and
his perceptible manifestations.

The first three *Sefiros* are חָכְמָה בִּינָה דַּעַת,
Wisdom, Understanding, Knowledge. A
person begins with חָכְמָה, the seed of
wisdom, the inspiration that is the father of
knowledge. But that first spark of knowledge
must be developed and applied properly —
that is בִּינָה, *understanding.* The first flash of
wisdom unites with the *understanding* which
develops that wisdom, to produce the firm
conclusions which constitute דַּעַת,
knowledge.

The next three *Sefiros* are חֶסֶד גְּבוּרָה
תִּפְאֶרֶת, *Kindness, Power, Splendor.*
Abraham was the embodiment of חֶסֶד,
kindness; Isaac represents גְּבוּרָה, *strength,*

and may He   *And they shall place My Name upon the Children of Israel, and I shall bless them.*

grant [to] you   *To You, HASHEM, is the Greatness and the Power and the Glory and the Eternality and the Splendor, even all that is in the heavens and the earth; to You, HASHEM, is the Kingdom and the sovereignty over every ruler.*

peace.   *"Peace, peace, to the far and to the near," says HASHEM, "and I shall heal him."*

---

alludes to three levels of peace: within the family, in the country where one lives, and throughout the world (*K'sav Sofer*).

It may seem to you that by devoting yourself exclusively to the service of God, you will cut yourself off from society and lose its friendship. God promises the contrary. If we make ourselves aware of His purpose, and seek to carry out His plan for the world, then all thoughtful and perceptive people will realize that we are making *their* world a better place, and they will seek to be at peace with us (*R' Hirsch*).

Peace is not simply the absence of war. It is a harmony between conflicting forces. Within man, it is the proper balance between the needs of the body and its higher duty to the soul. In the universe it is balance between the infinite elements as well as between the holy and the mundane. When Israel is sinful, it disrupts this balance because it is not making proper use of the human and physical resources God gives the world. This creates a barrier between God and His people, a barrier that God, with compassion, removes so that we can repent and return to the blessed condition of peaceful harmony (*Ohr HaChaim*; see also *Malbim*).

THE SECONDARY VERSES

strict judgment and avoidance of undeserved kindness; Jacob represents תִּפְאֶרֶת, *splendor.* The proper blend of חֶסֶד, *kindness*, and גְּבוּרָה, *strength*, produces תִּפְאֶרֶת, *splendor* (See Overviews to ArtScroll *Bereishis II and III*.)

The seventh *Sefirah* is נֵצַח, a word which can indicate either *Eternity* or *Triumph*. In a sense the two are related, because one who conquers adversity can endure. The eighth *Sefirah* is הוֹד, *Glory*. It opposes — or complements — the conquering aspect of the preceding emanation, just as *strength* is the counterpoint of *kindness*. Glory represents submission to circumstances rather than an attempt to conquer them. There are situations when one's greatest *glory* is acceptance of God's will as represented by the circumstances in which he has placed a person.

יְסוֹד, *Foundation*, is the ninth *Sefirah*. Since the emanations of the *Sefiros* go in descending order until they are finally actualized in creation, יְסוֹד, *Foundation*, also serves the harmonizing function of bringing together all of the preceding *Sefiros* enabling them to come into being in the physical world.

The next and last *Sefirah*, מַלְכוּת, *Kingship*, is the revelation of God's will in the material world, manifesting the final goal of God's sovereignty over the universe. [The discussion of the *Sefiros* as presented here is an abridged version of a much longer exposition in ArtScroll *Zemiros*, p. 226 ff.]

שָׁלוֹם שָׁלוֹם — *Peace, peace ...*

Great is peace for it is given to the true penitent — as it is written (*Isaiah* 57:19): *Peace, peace, to the far* [i.e., he who has strayed far away and returned] *and to the near* [i.e., the righteous one who did not stray] (*Sifre*).

[Perhaps this verse is cited as an allusion to the halachah that those present in the synagogue as well as those far out in the fields who cannot attend the services are included in the *Kohanim's* blessing. See p. 92 §12.]

יְהִי רָצוֹן מִלְּפָנֶיךָ, יהוה אֱלֹהַי וֵאלֹהֵי אֲבוֹתַי, שֶׁתַּעֲשֶׂה לְמַעַן קְדֻשַּׁת חֲסָדֶיךָ וְגֹדֶל רַחֲמֶיךָ הַפְּשׁוּטִים, וּלְמַעַן טָהֳרַת שִׁמְךָ הַגָּדוֹל הַגִּבּוֹר וְהַנּוֹרָא, בֶּן עֶשְׂרִים וּשְׁתַּיִם אוֹתִיּוֹת הַיּוֹצְאִים מִן הַפְּסוּקִים שֶׁל בִּרְכַּת כֹּהֲנִים

[אנקת"ם פסת"ם פספסי"ם דיונסי"ם]

הָאֲמוּרָה מִפִּי אַהֲרֹן וּבָנָיו עַם קְדוֹשֶׁךָ, שֶׁתִּהְיֶה קָרוֹב לִי בְּקָרְאִי לָךְ, וְתִשְׁמַע תְּפִלָּתִי נַאֲקָתִי וְאַנְקָתִי תָּמִיד, כְּשֵׁם שֶׁשָּׁמַעְתָּ אֶנְקַת יַעֲקֹב תְּמִימֶךָ הַנִּקְרָא אִישׁ תָּם.

וְתִתֶּן לִי וּלְכָל נַפְשׁוֹת בֵּיתִי מְזוֹנוֹתֵינוּ וּפַרְנָסָתֵנוּ — בְּרֶוַח וְלֹא בְצִמְצוּם, בְּהֶתֵּר וְלֹא בְאִסּוּר, בְּנַחַת וְלֹא בְצַעַר, — מִתַּחַת יָדְךָ הָרְחָבָה, כְּשֵׁם שֶׁנָּתַתָּ פִּסַּת לֶחֶם לֶאֱכֹל וּבֶגֶד לִלְבֹּשׁ לְיַעֲקֹב אָבִינוּ הַנִּקְרָא אִישׁ תָּם.

וְתִתְּנֵנוּ לְאַהֲבָה, לְחֵן וּלְחֶסֶד וּלְרַחֲמִים בְּעֵינֶיךָ וּבְעֵינֵי כָל רוֹאֵינוּ; וְיִהְיוּ דְבָרַי נִשְׁמָעִים לַעֲבוֹדָתֶךָ, כְּשֵׁם שֶׁנָּתַתָּ אֶת יוֹסֵף צַדִּיקֶךָ — בְּשָׁעָה שֶׁהִלְבִּישׁוֹ אָבִיו כְּתֹנֶת פַּסִּים — לְחֵן וּלְחֶסֶד וּלְרַחֲמִים בְּעֵינֶיךָ וּבְעֵינֵי כָל רוֹאָיו.

וְתַעֲשֶׂה עִמִּי נִפְלָאוֹת וְנִסִּים, וּלְטוֹבָה אוֹת, וְתַצְלִיחֵנִי בִּדְרָכַי, וְתֵן בְּלִבִּי בִּינָה לְהָבִין וּלְהַשְׂכִּיל וּלְקַיֵּם אֶת כָּל דִּבְרֵי תַלְמוּד תּוֹרָתֶךָ וְסוֹדוֹתֶיהָ; וְתַצִּילֵנִי מִשְּׁגִיאוֹת; וּתְטַהֵר רַעְיוֹנַי וְלִבִּי לַעֲבוֹדָתֶךָ וּלְיִרְאָתֶךָ. וְתַאֲרִיךְ יָמַי (וִימֵי אִשְׁתִּי וּבָנַי וּבְנוֹתַי וְאָבִי וְאִמִּי) בְּטוֹב וּבִנְעִימוֹת, בְּרֹב עֹז וְשָׁלוֹם, אָמֵן סֶלָה.

᳜ יְהִי רָצוֹן — **Second Supplication**
יְהִי רָצוֹן — *May it be acceptable.*

[Of comparatively recent origin, this prayer was first published about three centuries ago in *Shaarei Zion*. In many liturgies it came to replace the third recitation of the supplication regarding dreams. See preface to that prayer, p. 69.]

שִׁמְךָ ... בֶּן עֶשְׂרִים וּשְׁתַּיִם אוֹתִיּוֹת — *Your Name ... composed of twenty-two letters.*

See "The Divine Name of Twenty-two Letters", pp. 45-47.

כְּשֵׁם שֶׁנָּתַתָּ אֶת יוֹסֵף צַדִּיקֶךָ — *Just as You granted Joseph, Your righteous one.*

Joseph's example and his woolen tunic hardly seems to be an apt example of one who found favor, kindness and mercy in the eyes of all who beheld him. A simple reading of Scripture seems to indicate the opposite. As a result of Jacob preferring him over the other brothers — and, openly displaying that preference by garbing him distinctively — Joseph became the object of his brothers' hatred! [see *Genesis* 37:3-4].

The resolution of this contradiction lies in the term בְּשָׁעָה, *at the time*, which indicates that for a time, at the moment Jacob favored Joseph with this special garment, the brothers realized that Joseph *was* more worthy than them — otherwise Jacob would not have singled him out. But soon the brothers thought they detected a change in Joseph's attitude, thinking that he began acting

May it be acceptable before You, HASHEM my God and the God of my fathers, that You act for the sake of the holiness of Your loving-kindness and the greatness of Your mercies which reach out, and for the sake of the sanctity of Your Name — the great, the powerful and the awesome; composed of twenty-two letters which derive from the verses of Bircas Kohanim; spoken by Aaron and his sons, Your holy people — that You be near to me when I call to You; that You listen to my prayer, my plea and my cry at all times, just as You listened to the cry of Jacob, Your perfect one, who is called "a wholesome man."

And may You bestow upon me and upon all the souls of my household, our food and our sustenance — generously and not sparsely, honestly and not in forbidden fashion, pleasurably and not in pain — from beneath Your generous hand, just as You gave a portion of bread to eat and clothing to wear to our father Jacob who is called "a wholesome man."

And may You grant that we find love, favor, kindness and mercy in Your eyes and in the eyes of all who behold us; and that my words in Your service be heard; just as You granted Joseph, Your righteous one — at the time that his father garbed him in a fine woolen tunic — that he find favor, kindness and mercy in Your eyes and in the eyes of all who beheld him.

May You perform wonders and miracles with me, and a goodly sign; grant me success in my ways; place in my heart the power of understanding, to understand, to be wise, to fulfill all the words of Your Torah's teaching and its mysteries; save me from errors; and purify my thinking and my heart for Your service and Your awe. May You prolong my days (the appropriate words are inserted here: *and the days of my father, my mother, my wife, my sons, my daughters*) with goodness, with sweetness, with an abundance of strength and peace. Amen, Selah.

condescendingly toward them. They interpreted his every action as self-aggrandizement, and this turned them against him. For a period he had been worthy, they admitted, but no longer. Therefore, they hated him.

In truth, Joseph continued to find favor in the eyes of all who beheld him impartially, not as siblings [see *Overview*, ArtScroll *Bereishis*, pp. 1574 ff.]. The Torah bears witness to Joseph's standing in the eyes of his beholders: *His master perceived that HASHEM was with him ... Joseph found favor in his eyes (Genesis 39:3-4,); HASHEM was with Joseph ... He made the prison warden view him favorably (ibid. v. 21); and, Pharoah said to his servants, 'Could we find another like him — a man in whom is the spirit of God?' (ibid. 41-38).* That his brothers did not also see Joseph in this light can only be attributed to Divine intervention which was paving the way for Jacob's descent to Egypt and the eventual redemption (*VeAni Sefillah*).

וְתַעֲשֶׂה עִמִּי נִפְלָאוֹת וְנִסִּים — *May You perform wonders and miracles with me.*

It is unseemly for an individual to request miraculous intervention in his personal affairs, for what assurance does he have that he is deserving? On behalf of the community, however, one may request miracles; certainly the combined merits of many individuals make the group deserving. For this reason B'chor Shor (cited in Anaf Yosef) emends this reading to וְתַעֲשֶׂה לָנוּ, and performs for us.

Bechor Shor also offers an alternative resolution to justify the original wording. There are two classifications of miracle: overt [e.g., the splitting of the Sea of Reeds; Joshua's stopping the sun] and covert [e.g., the seeming historic simplicity of the Purim story]. It is wrong for an individual to request obvious miracles, but he may pray for covert miracles, because they are disguised as natural phenomena.

וְשָׂמוּ אֶת שְׁמִי — Scripture's Concluding Verse

After the three verses of the Priestly Blessing, the Torah concludes: וְשָׂמוּ אֶת שְׁמִי עַל־בְּנֵי יִשְׂרָאֵל, וַאֲנִי אֲבָרְכֵם, And they shall place My Name upon the Children of Israel and I shall bless them (Numbers 6:27).

וְשָׂמוּ אֶת שְׁמִי — And they shall place My Name.

In reciting the blessings [in the Temple] the Kohanim are to pronounce God's Ineffable Name (Sifre).

The Kohanim are to sanctify Israel with the holiness represented by God's Name — then the people will be truly worthy of blessing. Alternatively, the Kohanim have already incorporated God's Name into their blessings — since each verse of the blessings contains the name HASHEM. Consequently the people will be blessed by God (Ibn Ezra).

The Kohanim 'place' God's Name upon Israel by proclaiming that He is the source of all blessings (Ha'amek Davar); and by stamping upon us the awareness that every gift is a revelation of His will (R' Hirsch).

וַאֲנִי אֲבָרְכֵם — And I shall bless them.

R' Yishmael says: We have learned that a blessing is pronounced upon Israel by the Kohanim, but we have not learned that there is a blessing for the Kohanim themselves. When it says and I shall bless them — you are to understand that the Kohanim bless Israel, and the Holy One, Blessed is He, blesses the Kohanim.

R' Akiva says: We have learned that there is a blessing for Israel pronounced by the Kohanim, but [that Israel is blessed] by the Almighty we have not learned. When it says and I shall bless them, you are to understand that the Kohanim bless Israel and the Holy One, Blessed is He, ratifies what they have done. But [if so], how does R' Akiva derive a blessing for the Kohanim? R' Nachman bar Yitzchak said: [From the verse (Genesis 12:3)] and I [i.e., God will bless those who bless you we know that the Kohanim who bless Israel are surely entitled to a blessing (Chullin 49a).

When we are told that He will bless them, it is not clear whom God will bless — Israel or the Kohanim. The word them may also refer to all of them; God will bless both the Kohanim and the entire nation (Ibn Ezra).

At the conclusion of the blessing, Scripture stresses that while the Kohanim have pronounced the words of the blessing, only God can bless (R' Hirsch).

All the pleasures of this world are not true blessings, because people become bored with them and every thinking person comes to realize that life must have some purpose greater than the accumulation of money and enjoyment. The true blessings can be only the spiritual ones of the World to Come. If the Kohanim succeed in placing 'God's Name' upon the people by making them realize what truly matters — then God promises to give us the blessings of the World to Come (Chasam Sofer).

⊷§ עָשִׂינוּ מַה שֶּׁגָּזְרְתָּ — The Kohen's Concluding Prayer

This closing prayer by the *Kohanim* that their blessing be accepted and reinforced by God is found in its entirety in the Talmud *(Sotah 39a)*: 'When the *Kohen* turns his face from the congregation [after finishing the blessings he turns to face the Ark until the *chazzan* completes *Sim Shalom (Rashi)*] and says, 'Master of the world ...'

This prayer should be recited slowly so that it is concluded simultaneously with the *chazzan's* completion of *Sim Shalom*. Thus the congregation's *amen* will apply to both the *chazzan's* blessing and the *Kohanim's* prayer *(Rashi, Sotah 39b)*.

If a *Kohen* completes this prayer before the *chazzan* reaches the end of *Sim Shalom*, he should add *Adir BaMarom* to his prayer so that he and the *chazzan* will conclude simultaneously. Then, the *amen* will apply to both, as above *(Ramah 128:15)*.

On Rosh Hashanah and Yom Kippur when additional prayers such as the *piyut* הַיּוֹם תְּאַמְצֵנוּ, *On this day — strengthen us,* are added before the end of *Sim Shalom*, the *Kohanim* should not begin this prayer until just before the *piyut* ends. In this way they will conclude in time for the communal *amen (Mishnah Berurah 128:54)*.

The *Kohanim* may not turn their faces [from the people] until the *chazzan* has begun *Sim Shalom*. And they may not lower their hands until they have turned their faces. They must stand in their places [silently *(Mishnah Berurah)*] and not move from there until the *chazzan* completes *Sim Shalom*. Some maintain that they must wait until the congregation has finished the *amen* response after *Sim Shalom*. This is the prevalent custom *(Shulchan Aruch 128:45 and Rama)*.

Since it is customary today to say יִשַׁר כֹּחַךְ, *may your strength be aligned* [a blessing often given as an expression of gratitude to one who has performed a *mitzvah* or done someone a favor; in this case the *Kohen* has done both], it is preferable for the *Kohanim* to remain in their places on the *duchan* until after the *chazzan's* recital of *Kaddish*. Otherwise, many people, in their haste to show their appreciation, will be distracted from responding to the *Kaddish (Mishnah Berurah 128:60)*.

Upon descending the *duchan*, the *Kohen* should not turn his back to the Ark, but should back away with his face partially facing the Ark, as a respectful disciple would do when taking leave of his master *(Mishnah Berurah 128:61)*. After descending, the *Kohen* should not touch his shoes with his hands until he has finished the remaining prayers. If he does touch his shoes, he should wash his hands before continuing *(Rama 128:17)*.

⊷§ אַדִּיר בַּמָּרוֹם — The Congregation's Concluding Prayer

In most communities the congregation recites אַדִּיר בַּמָּרוֹם, *Mighty One on High,* while the *chazzan* says *Sim Shalom*. The individual should pace himself to finish אַדִּיר בַּמָּרוֹם simultaneously with the *chazzan's* conclusion of *Sim Shalom*, thus enabling the communal *amen* to apply to his prayer also *(Taz 130:2; see also Rama 130:1, Mishnah Berurah 130:10)*.

Additionally on days when the *Kohanim* do not ascend the *duchan* but *Bircas Kohanim* is recited by the *chazzon*, the congregation should recite *Adir BaMarom* while the *chazzan* says *Sim Shalom*, and its conclusion should coincide with the *chazzan's (Rama 130:1)*.

The text of this prayer as recorded in the Talmud is shorter than the version presently prevalent. The Talmud's version omits the words וְעַל כָּל עַמְּךְ בֵּית יִשְׂרָאֵל חַיִּים וּבְרָכָה לְמִשְׁמֶרֶת, *and all of Your people, the house of Israel, life and blessing for a safeguard of [peace]*.

The chazzan immediately begins שִׁים שָׁלוֹם. Then the Kohanim turn back to the Ark, lower their hands and recite their concluding prayer רִבּוֹנוֹ שֶׁל עוֹלָם. Meanwhile the congregation recites אַדִּיר בַּמָּרוֹם. All should conclude their respective prayers simultaneously with the chazzan's conclusion of שִׁים שָׁלוֹם.

רִבּוֹנוֹ שֶׁל עוֹלָם, עָשִׂינוּ מַה שֶׁגָּזַרְתָּ עָלֵינוּ, אַף אַתָּה עֲשֵׂה עִמָּנוּ כְּמָה שֶׁהִבְטַחְתָּנוּ: הַשְׁקִיפָה מִמְּעוֹן קָדְשְׁךָ, מִן הַשָּׁמַיִם, וּבָרֵךְ אֶת עַמְּךָ אֶת יִשְׂרָאֵל, וְאֵת הָאֲדָמָה אֲשֶׁר נָתַתָּה לָנוּ — כַּאֲשֶׁר נִשְׁבַּעְתָּ לַאֲבוֹתֵינוּ — אֶרֶץ זָבַת חָלָב וּדְבָשׁ.

אַדִּיר בַּמָּרוֹם, שׁוֹכֵן בִּגְבוּרָה, אַתָּה שָׁלוֹם וְשִׁמְךָ שָׁלוֹם. יְהִי רָצוֹן שֶׁתָּשִׂים עָלֵינוּ וְעַל כָּל עַמְּךָ בֵּית יִשְׂרָאֵל חַיִּים וּבְרָכָה לְמִשְׁמֶרֶת שָׁלוֹם.

עָשִׂינוּ מַה שֶׁגָּזַרְתָּ עָלֵינוּ — *We have done what You have decreed upon us.*

The blessing recited prior to *Bircas Kohanim* describes it as a 'command' — וְצִוָּנוּ, *and* [He has] *commanded us.* If so, why does this declaration describe it as a גְּזֵרָה, *decree?*

Baruch She'amar explains the change by citing the Talmud's (*Chullin* 49a) comment that God promises to reinforce the blessing issued by the *Kohanim.* Since God promises to reinforce the words of the *Kohanim* — and, in any event, no blessing of any sort is effective without Him — the agency of the *Kohanim* would seem to be superfluous; why should not God give these blessings directly? The manner of *Bircas Kohanim* would seem to be like other *mitzvos* that are not comprehensible to human intelligence. Concerning such *mitzvos,* the Sages use the dictum (*Yoma* 67b): 'I am HASHEM! I have decreed (גְּזַרְתִּיו) it to be so! You have no right to question me!'

So too in our case, although the *Kohanim* may not understand the need for their pronouncement they, nevertheless, issue it wholeheartedly because גָּזַרְתָּ עָלֵינוּ, *You have decreed upon us.*

הַשְׁקִיפָה מִמְּעוֹן קָדְשְׁךָ — *Look down from Your sacred dwelling ...*

[This verse appears in Scripture (*Deuteronomy* 26:15) as the closing words of the declaration one recites

upon removing from his house of any remaining tithes that he had failed to distribute before Pesach of the third and sixth years of the Sabbatical cycle: ... *I have hearkened to the voice of HASHEM, my God; I have acted in accordance with all that You have commanded me. 'Look down from Your sacred dwelling' and bless Your people Israel ...* (*Deuteronomy* 26:14-15). Regarding *Bircas Kohanim* this verse has the same import — the *Kohanim* invoke God's promise to the Patriarchs in response to their fulfillment of His commandment.]

וּבָרֵךְ אֶת עַמְּךָ אֶת יִשְׂרָאֵל — *And bless Your people, Israel ...*

... with sons and daughters (*Sifre*).

The redundant *Your people, Israel,* is explained by *Malbim* as a condition to the requested blessing. *Bless Your people,* but only if they follow in the path of *Israel* [i.e., Jacob]. This is reminiscent of the blessing which Israel (Jacob) himself gave to Menasheh and Ephraim the sons of Joseph: *May the angel who redeems me from all evil bless the lads and may He call them with My Name and the names of my fathers, Abraham and Isaac; and may they increase like fish within the earth* (*Genesis* 48:16). Jacob made his blessing of fruitfulness dependent upon Menasheh and Ephraim following in the footsteps of the Patriarchs, thus earning the right to be called by their name.

Order of Bircas Kohanim [86]

The chazzan *immediately begins* שִׂים שָׁלוֹם. *Then the* Kohanim *turn back to the Ark, lower their hands and recite their concluding prayer* רִבּוֹנוֹ שֶׁל עוֹלָם. *Meanwhile the congregation recites* אַדִּיר בַּמָּרוֹם. *All should conclude their respective prayers simultaneously with the* chazzan's *conclusion of* שִׂים שָׁלוֹם.

Master of the world, we have done what You have decreed upon us, now may You also do as You have promised us: Look down from Your sacred dwelling, from the heavens, and bless Your people, Israel, and the earth which You have given us — just as You have sworn to our fathers — a land that flows with milk and honey.

Mighty One on high, He Who dwells in power! You are Peace and Your Name is Peace! May it be acceptable that You grant us and all of Your people, the house of Israel, life and blessing for a safeguard of peace.

אַדִּיר בַּמָּרוֹם — *Mighty One on high.*
This descriptive praise of the Creator is from *Psalms* (93:4): *More the roars of many waters, mightier than the waves of the sea*, אַדִּיר בַּמָּרוֹם ה׳, *You are the Mighty One on high, O HASHEM.* According to the Midrash (*Bereishis Rabbah* 5:1), it was the very first expression of exaltation ever used during creation of the world. After the waters were brought into being they sang God's praise with the words *You are the Mighty One on high, O HASHEM.* Upon hearing their song, the Holy One, Blessed is He, said, 'If these, which have neither mouth nor speech praise Me in this manner, how much more so will man, whom I will shortly create!'

שׁוֹכֵן בִּגְבוּרָה — *He Who dwells in power.*
This term of praise is late in origin and is not found in Scripture (*Tikkun Tefillah*).

אַתָּה שָׁלוֹם וְשִׁמְךָ שָׁלוֹם — *You are Peace and Your Name is Peace.*
The word בָּרוּךְ at the beginning of a blessing is usually translated *blessed*. But the word conveys the much deeper concept of God as מְקוֹר הַבְּרָכוֹת, *the Source of all blessings.* Similarly רַחוּם does not describe God merely as the *Merciful One*, but as the wellspring from which all mercy issues (*The World of Prayer*).

[The term שָׁלוֹם should also be interpreted in this light. *You are Peace —* all peace in the universe is from You. But in a larger sense שָׁלוֹם has an even greater connotation. Unlike בָּרוּךְ, *blessed*, and רַחוּם, *merciful*, which are descriptive adjectives, the word שָׁלוֹם is a proper noun — one of the Divine appellations which may not be pronounced in a degrading manner or in a place of defilement.] The Talmud (*Shabbos* 10b) teaches that one may not offer his friend the commonplace greeting of שָׁלוֹם עֲלֵיכֶם [*Shalom aleichem*], usually rendered *peace unto you*, in a bathhouse where people stand unclothed. This ruling is based on the verse, *And he* [Gideon] *called Him, HASHEM Shalom (Judges* 6:24). Thus the greeting means more than 'Peace be with You'; it contains the deeper implication of 'God of Peace be with you', and it is unseemly to mention the Divine Name in a place where people stand unclothed.

Thus our phrase should be understood as, *You are the source of all peace, moreover, Your very Name is Peace.*]

חַיִּים וּבְרָכָה לְמִשְׁמֶרֶת שָׁלוֹם — *Life and blessing for a safeguard of peace.*
Tikkun Tefillah explains this as the blessing of an abundant food supply, which not only sustains life but also safeguards peace. This is based on the Talmudic dictum: A person should always be careful to have grain in his house, for strife is not found in any

שִׂים שָׁלוֹם, טוֹבָה וּבְרָכָה, חֵן וָחֶסֶד
וְרַחֲמִים, עָלֵינוּ וְעַל כָּל
יִשְׂרָאֵל עַמֶּךָ. בָּרְכֵנוּ אָבִינוּ, כֻּלָּנוּ כְּאֶחָד, בְּאוֹר
פָּנֶיךָ; כִּי בְאוֹר פָּנֶיךָ נָתַתָּ לָנוּ, יהוה אֱלֹהֵינוּ,
תּוֹרַת חַיִּים וְאַהֲבַת חֶסֶד, וּצְדָקָה וּבְרָכָה
וְרַחֲמִים, וְחַיִּים וְשָׁלוֹם. וְטוֹב בְּעֵינֶיךָ לְבָרֵךְ אֶת
עַמְּךָ יִשְׂרָאֵל בְּכָל עֵת וּבְכָל שָׁעָה בִּשְׁלוֹמֶךָ. בָּרוּךְ
אַתָּה, יהוה, הַמְבָרֵךְ אֶת עַמּוֹ יִשְׂרָאֵל בַּשָּׁלוֹם:

man's home except regarding grain-stuffs ... This is the meaning of the folk saying, 'When the urn has been emptied of its barley, dispute knocks and enters' (Bava Metzia 59a).

⦿§ שִׂים שָׁלוֹם — Set Peace

The concluding blessing of Shemoneh Esrei is a request for peace, for, as we have seen above, the Sages regard peace as the ultimate blessing, the one without which no other blessing has permanence. That this prayer begins its list of request with peace is not only indicative of that blessing's paramount role in life, but it is also a direct allusion to Bircas Kohanim. The last blessing of the Kohanim was that God grant Israel peace — we now continue Shemoneh Esrei with mention of

that very blessing (Vilna Gaon).

The prayer begins with a list of six blessings. As the Sages teach, peace is the prerequisite blessing — the vessel that contains all other good things. We ask for it first, because one must first be sure his 'vessel' is in good repair before he can fill it with assorted bounty (Iyun Tefillah).

The six forms of goodness listed here — peace, goodness, blessing, graciousness, kindness, and compassion — allude to the six blessings of Bircas Kohanim (Etz Yosef).

חֵן וָחֶסֶד וְרַחֲמִים — Graciousness, kindness and compassion.

Man goes through stages of development in life. Sometimes he is growing and improving — then he is deserving of

*S*et peace, goodness, blessing, graciousness, kindness and compassion upon us and all of Israel, Your people. Bless us, our Father, all of us equally with the light of Your face, for with the light of Your face you gave us the Torah of life and a love of kindness, and righteousness, blessing, compassion, life and peace. May it be good in Your eyes to bless Your people Israel in every season and in every hour with Your peace. Blessed are You HASHEM, who blesses His people Israel with peace.

God's *graciousness*. Sometimes man is in a period of maturity, when he does not improve, but continues the accomplishments of his more fruitful period — then God grants him *kindness*. Sometimes he declines and does not deserve God's help — but even then God shows *compassion (Ikkarim).*

כֻּלָנוּ כְּאֶחָד — *All of us equally.*
Israel reaches its highest potential when all Jews receive an equal share of blessing. Specifically, we ask that God give us all the *light of His face*, meaning the ability to understand His ways and our mission is attaining His goals for the world (R' Hirsch).

כִּי בְאוֹר פָּנֶיךָ נָתַתָּ לָנוּ ... — *For with the light of Your face.*
Even in earliest times, the nation reached the pinnacle of greatness only because God chose to reveal Himself to us. He gave us the Torah as an act of kindness, not because we were worthy of its indescribable spiritual riches (*Iyun Tefillah*).

תּוֹרַת חַיִים — *The Torah of life.*
Far from being a burden, the Torah gives, insures, and enriches life.

וְאַהֲבַת חֶסֶד — *And a love of kindness.*
God is not content if we merely act kindly toward others. He wants us to *love* kindness. What someone loves to do is never a chore (*Chafetz Chaim*).
Alternatively, God gave us *undeserved* love, i.e., His abundant love for Israel is a manifestation of His חֶסֶד, kindness (*Iyun Tefillah*).

✑ Laws of Bircas Kohanim

The halachos [laws] of Bircas Kohanim are discussed in chapters 128-130 of Shulchan Aruch Orach Chaim. For the reader's convenience, the laws pertaining directly to the procedure of the blessings have been inserted in the order of Bircas Kohanim, as introductory essays, or in the commentary. A selection of the remaining halachos are presented here. Unless otherwise noted, they have been culled from chapter 128 of Shulchan Aruch Orach Chaim [here abbreviated SA] or one of Chofetz Chaim's three commentaries to that work: Mishnah Berurah [MB], Be'ur Halachah [BH], and Shaar HaTziyun [SH].

1. Bircas Kohanim is a Scripturally ordained positive mitzvah [מִצְוַת עֲשֵׂה מִדְאוֹרַיְיתָא] incumbent upon every Kohen, both in Eretz Yisrael and elsewhere (SH, footnote to 44). Any Kohen in the synagogue who does not ascend the duchan [platform from which the Blessing is pronounced] is in violation of this mitzvah, unless he is excused or disqualified by the Halachah. By his refusal to ascend, the Kohen transgresses one mitzvah which is reckoned as three mitzvos (Numbers 6:23,27); כֹּה תְבָרֲכוּ, So shall you bless; אָמוֹר לָהֶם, Saying to them; and וְשָׂמוּ אֶת שְׁמִי, Let them place My Name (SA 2; MB 8). However, a Kohen is not required to ascend the duchan unless he was present when the chazzan issued the general call, 'Kohanim', or he was personally asked [by a representative of the congregation] to ascend or to wash his hands preparatory to reciting the blessings (SA 2).

According to Sefer Chareidim the mitzvah is fulfilled not only by the Kohanim, but also by 'the members of the congregation who stand silently facing the Kohanim and concentrate on receiving the blessing as commanded by God' (preface to BH). [See, however, Ritva (Succah 31b), who maintains that the mitzvah applies only to Kohanim.]

2. A minyan [quorum] of ten adult males is necessary for Bircas Kohanim. The Kohanim are included in the quorum even if they constitute a majority of the congregation (SA 1; MB 2). In a congregation composed of Kohanim exclusively, the following procedures are followed: If it consists of exactly ten Kohanim, nine of them ascend the duchan, while the tenth — the chazzan — remains at his post and calls out the words to them. If the congregation is larger, then a total of ten Kohanim — the chazzan and nine others — remain in their places to 'receive' the blessings and answer amen. The other Kohanim ascend the duchan to pronounce Bircas Kohanim (SA 25; MB 97, 99).

If the chazzan began his repetition of Shemoneh Esrei in the presence of the required minyan [quorum of ten males over bar mitzvah age], but some of them subsequently left the synagogue leaving less than ten men behind, the chazzan may continue his recital provided at least six, including himself, are present. He may not begin Bircas Kohanim with less than a minyan, however. If ten were present when the Kohanim began pronouncing the blessing, they may continue even if some walked out, provided at least six remained (MB 1; BH, s.v. בפחות).

3. Once he has pronounced Bircas Kohanim on a particular day, a Kohen is not required to recite it again that day, even if a congregation asks him to do so (SA 3).

Nevertheless, such a Kohen may volunteer to ascend the duchan a second time if he so wishes (SA 28), in which case he must repeat the prior blessing, '... Who has sanctified us with the holiness of Aaron ...' (MB 11, 106).

4. A Kohen who has not yet recited Shemoneh Esrei when the congregation is up to Bircas Kohanim, should ascend the *duchan*, for his own *Shemoneh Esrei* prayer is not a necessary precondition to the recitation of *Bircas Kohanim (SA 29).*

But if the *Kohen* realizes that *Bircas Kohanim* will force him to miss the deadline for his *Shemoneh Esrei*, he should leave the synagogue and recite his own prayers outside. However, if he was personally asked to ascend the *duchan*, he should do so, because the requirement to pronounce *Bircas Kohanim* when summoned is a Scriptural commandment, while the recitation of *Shemoneh Esrei* is a *mitzvah* of Rabbinic origin.

If he has not yet recited the *Shema* and realizes that the proper time for its recital will soon elapse, he should likewise step outside and recite the *Shema*. If, however, he has been called to ascend, he should recite only the first verse of *Shema* and then ascend *(MB 107).*

5. Regarding a *Kohen* who has begun *Shemoneh Esrei* and realizes that he will not finish before the *chazzan* reaches *Bircas Kohanim:*

(a) If other *Kohanim* are present, he may not interrupt his prayers for *Bircas Kohanim;*

(b) even though other *Kohanim* are present, if the praying *Kohen* was personally asked to ascend or to wash his hands, he must interrupt his prayers and join the other *Kohanim* in blessing the congregation; then he returns to his place to finish *Shemoneh Esrei;*

(c) if no other Kohanim are present, many authorities require him to interrupt his prayers whether or not he was personally asked to ascend. In such a situation the *Kohen* should move his feet slightly forward when the *chazzan* recites רְצֵה. He should also attempt to reach שִׁים שָׁלוֹם — the point where *Bircas Kohanim* is recited — by the time the *chazzan* reaches that blessing. Nevertheless, even if he does not reach שִׁים שָׁלוֹם, these authorities permit him to interrupt his prayers and ascend the duchan. If the *Kohen* feels that he will become confused and be unable to

return to his place in *Shemoneh Esrei* he should not ascend unless personally asked to do so.

Other authorities do not permit a *Kohen* to interrupt his *Shmoneh Esrei* unless two conditions are met: (a) He is certain that he will be able to return to his own prayers; and (b) he has reached שִׁים שָׁלוֹם in his *Shemoneh Esrei (MB 106; SH 83).*

6. The *Kohanim* may not ascend the *duchan* wearing shoes, whether of leather or of other material.

The shoes should not be left conspicuously in the synagogue, for this shows disrespect for the congregation. They should be put out of sight, in a corner or under a bench. The prohibition applies equally to shoes of materials other than leather, whether they are laced or slipped-on.

Since in today's age people are not accustomed to going barefoot, the *Kohanim* should wear cloth socks when they stand before the congregation *(SA 5; MB 15, 17-18).*

7. Even though the *Kohanim* washed their hands ritually [נְטִילַת יָדַיִם] in the morning [i.e., before the prayers], they must rewash their hands — until the wrist — before ascending the *duchan* (SA 6).

Although in some instances where washing is required halachically, it is sufficient to clean the hands thoroughly with a medium other than water, for example, by rubbing them with clean dry sand; nevertheless, for *Bircas Kohanim*, only water is acceptable *(MB 19).*

Many authorities require that this washing be done with clear water poured by human hands from a utensil with a volume of a *revi'is* [from 3.3 — 5.5 ounces] *(MB 21).*

If no water is available, *Kohanim* who washed their hands earlier in the day and were scrupulous not to touch anything dirty may rely on *Rambam's* view that rewashing is not required *(MB 20).*

8. If the *Kohen* recited the blessing עַל נְטִילַת יָדַיִם after washing his hands in the morning, he should not repeat that blessing when washing his hands before *Bircas Kohanim* (*SA 7*). However, some authorities hold that only if the hands were kept uncontaminated should the *Kohanim* not recite a blessing upon washing them before *Bircas Kohanim*. It is advisable, therefore, for a *Kohen* to scrupulously avoid any contact with unclean substances from morning until *Bircas Kohanim* (*MB 24*).

9. The *Kohen's* hands should be washed by a Levite (*SA 6*).[1]

If no Levite is present the washing should be done by a firstborn man (i.e. a male who is his mother's first conceived child). If no firstborn is present either, then the *Kohen* should wash his own hands (*MB 22*).

Even if the Levite is a Torah scholar and the *Kohen* is an ignoramus, it is preferable that the Levite pour the water on the *Kohen's* hands (*MB 22*).

Although in some communities the Levites wash their own hands before pouring water on the *Kohen's* this is not the prevalent custom (*SA and Rama 6*).

However, if the Levites were not scrupulous in avoiding unclean matter during the interim, and especially if they touched any part of the body usually kept covered, it is preferable that they wash their hands anew (*MB 23*).

10. *Bircas Kohanim* does not override the Scriptural prohibition forbidding a *Kohen* from being under the same roof as a corpse. Thus, if — Heaven forbid — someone dies in the synagogue, the *Kohanim* must be told to leave even if the *chazzan* has summoned them to pronounce the blessings (*MB 8*).

11. *Kohanim* should not change their chant during *Bircas* *Kohanim* in order to avoid confusing themselves or the *chazzan*. For the same reason, all *Kohanim* in the group on the *duchan* should sing the same tune (*SA 21; MB 82, 84*).

[In most communities the tunes are centuries-old. While in many places the same chant is used every time the *Kohanim* ascend the *duchan*, some communities (e.g., Frankfurt am Main, Pressburg) have a special tune for each festival.]

12. People standing behind the *Kohanim* — even if they are not directly behind, but behind them toward the side — do not receive the benefits of the blessing, because the *Kohanim* and congregation must face one another. This is so even if no partition is between them (*SA 24; MB 93, 94*).

Those who stand in front of, or even alongside the *Kohanim*, are included in the blessing. All members of the congregation, wherever they are standing, should turn to face the *Kohanim* (*MB 95*).

Those members of the congregation who usually sit along the eastern wall of the synagogue would be *behind* the *Kohanim*, who are in front of the Ark. They should leave their places, therefore, to stand in front of the *Kohanim*, otherwise they would not be included in the blessing (*MB 95*). However, people who are unable to be in the synagogue [those working in the fields, or those incapacitated by sickness] *are* included in the blessing (*SA 24*).

Although the blessing *does* apply to people who cannot be in the synagogue to stand before the *Kohanim*, this dispensation does not apply to people in the synagogue and who remain behind the *Kohanim*. By this blatant disregard for the sanctity of the blessing, such people exclude themselves (*MB 96*). The same applies to people who could easily attend the synagogue, but do not care to do so (*BH, s.v.* אם הם).

---

1. In the Frankfurt am Main community, the washing is performed very ceremoniously at the front of the synagogue with silver washing vessels, in order to glorify the *mitzvah*.

13. In the case of other prayers and blessings, it is forbidden to recite them or respond to them in the presence of a foul odor. This applies to *Bircas Kohanim* as well *(BH, s.v. אפילו)*.

14. The *Kohanim* do not recite any word of the blessing until they hear it from the *chazzan (SA 18)*. This reading of the words should preferably not be done by a fellow *Kohen*. It is desirable that a non-*Kohen* be selected as *chazzan*, if possible *(MB 85)*. If no other member of the congregation is qualified to serve as *chazzan* or to read before the *Kohanim*, then a *Kohen* may be *chazzan* and may read before his fellow *Kohanim (MB 87)*.

15. If a *Kohen* is the *chazzan*, and there are other *Kohanim* present, he should not raise his hands *(SA 20)*. He should not be asked to ascend the *duchan* or to wash his hands, for if he is asked he must do so *(Rama 20)*. A non-*Kohen* should stand next to him, issue the call, 'Kohanim', and read the words of *Bircas Kohanim* for them, while the *chazzan* stands silently in his place *(SA 22)* until the conclusion of *Bircas Kohanim*. The *chazzan* then continues שִׂים שָׁלוֹם *(MB 87)*.

If the *chazzan* is the only *Kohen* present, he may raise his hands rather than have *Bircas Kohanim* neglected entirely. He should step slightly forward during the blessing of רְצֵה, and continue saying until the end of the מוֹדִים. Then he should ascend the *duchan*, face the congregation, recite *Bircas Kohanim*, including the prior blessing, with another person reading the words before him. After *Bircas Kohanim* he should return to his place and recite שִׂים שָׁלוֹם *(SA 20; MB 77-79)*.

16. In many communities, it is customary for the congregation to show appreciation to the *Kohanim* by greeting them with the salutation, 'יִישַׁר כֹּחֲךָ, may your strength be aligned' [i.e., may you continue to be able to perform *mitzvos*], as they descend the *duchan*. However, this should not be done until

the *chazzan* has finished *Shemoneh Esrei* and *Kaddish*; otherwise the tumult would disrupt the prayers. To avoid such disruption, the *Kohanim* do not leave the *duchan* until after *Kaddish (MB 60)*.

17. A *Kohen* whose hand or face is blemished or deformed in such a way that the congregation will be distracted from concentrating on the words of the blessing should not raise his hands. The same applies to a *Kohen* with uncontrollable drooling or tearing *(SA 30; MB 109)*.

One who is blind, even in only one eye, should not ascend the *duchan (SA 30)*, unless his blindness is not obvious to the onlooker *(BH, s.v. וכן סומא)*.

The same disqualification applies to one who is discolored by paint or dye *(SA 32)*.

It is preferable that *Kohanim* disqualified because of such imperfections not remain in the synagogue during *Bircas Kohanim*. If one afflicted with any of these imperfections has ascended the *duchan*, however, he need not descend *(BH, s.v. מי שיש)*.

The above laws apply to townspeople who will not be distracted by his imperfections. Even if he is blind in both eyes, he may raise his hands *(SA 30)*.

18. It has become customary for each *Kohen* to drape his *tallis* over his face while pronouncing *Bircas Kohanim*. Many *Kohanim* drape the *tallis* over their outstretched fingers as well, thus preventing the congregation from staring at them during the blessing. In communities where this practice is followed, imperfections on the hands or face do not disqualify a *Kohen* since they are covered by his *tallis* and the congregation cannot stare at them *(SA 31)*.

19. A *Kohen* with stomach disorders should not ascend the *duchan* but should preferably leave the synagogue before the *chazzan* reaches רְצֵה *(MB 111)*.

20. One who stutters, stammers, lisps or otherwise does not enunciate clearly should not ascend the duchan (SA 33; MB 119). If a significant minority of a particular area mispronounces a letter — in some parts of Russia many people do not differentiate between *sh* and *s* — some authorities permit such *Kohanim* to ascend the duchan in that locality (MB 119).

21. Someone under *bar mitzvah* may not pronounce *Bircas Kohanim* if he is the only *Kohen* present, because an entire congregation should not depend on the blessing of a child (SA 34; MB 12). Together with adult *Kohanim*, however, he may ascend the duchan, so that he will become fluent and experienced by the time he comes of age (SA 34; MB 123).

22. Although a *Kohen* who took a life, even inadvertently, may not ascend the duchan (SA 35), this disqualification does not apply in a case where a *Kohen* circumcized a baby, and the baby died (SA 36). Firstly, his intentions were to perform a *mitzvah*. Also, it is possible that the baby was not fully developed. Additionally, the death was not necessarily due to the circumcision (MB 132).

23. One who has converted to a different faith may not raise his hands. Some authorities maintain that if he has repented he may raise his hands. If his conversion were forced, all agree that he may raise his hands in blessing (SA 37).

One who has promised to convert but returned to Judaism before fulfilling his word is not disqualified according to either view (MB 134).

24. A *Kohen* who drank a *revi'is* of wine — as little as 3.3 ounces according to some authorities — in one quaff may not raise his hands, but if he drank the *revi'is* in two quaffs or diluted it with water, he is permitted to raise his hands. If he drank more than a *revi'is*, even if it had been diluted or had been drunk in several quaffs, he may not raise his hands until the effects of the wine have passed (SA 38).

Many authorities do not differentiate between wine and other alcoholic beverages (MB 141).

25. A *Kohen* may pronounce the blessings even if he is not scrupulous in the general performance of *mitzvos* (other than conversion and bloodshed), and even if the people accuse him of sinfulness. He *is* disqualified, however, if he is guilty of desecrating his *Kehunah* by contaminating himself to the dead or marrying a woman forbidden to a *Kohen* (SA 39; MB 145; see laws 27-28 below).

Rambam explains why a sinner is permitted to bless the nation. Since *Bircas Kohanim* is a positive Scriptural command incumbent upon every *Kohen* we may not say to a sinner (who is not otherwise disqualified), 'Add to your evil ways by not fulfilling yet another *mitzvah.*' In any case, the efficacy of the blessing is not dependent upon the *Kohanim* but upon the Holy One, Blessed is He — as the verse states: *And they shall place My Name upon the Children of Israel, and I shall bless them.* The *Kohanim* do what is commanded of them and the Holy One, Blessed is He, in His mercy, will bless Israel according to His will (MB 146).

26. One who has married a divorcee or any other woman forbidden to a *Kohen* may not raise his hands, nor is he accorded such honors as being called first to the Torah. Even if he divorces her or if she dies, he is still disqualified until he vows, under public authority [עַל דַּעַת רַבִּים], never again to have relations with women forbidden him as a *Kohen* (SA 40; MB 147).

One who was born to a *Kohen* who married such a women is called a *challal* [desecrated one] and is forbidden to ascend the duchan (SA 42; MB 155).

27. A *Kohen* who has intentionally become contaminated by a dead body is disqualified from ascending the *duchan* and from all other prerogatives of *Kohanim* until he has repented and agreed never to do so again. This does not apply to the bodies of the seven relatives — parents, children, brother, unmarried sister, and spouse — whom a *Kohen* is commanded to honor in death (*SA* 41).

It is probable that this rule applies only to a *Kohen* who habitually allows himself to become contaminated. But one who allowed himself to become contaminated one time need not be disqualified on this account. This situation is not similar to a *Kohen* who *continuously* lives with a forbidden wife (*BH*, s.v. נטמא למת).

Proper repentance in this case requires merely that he declare before the *beis din* his readiness to refrain from further contamination. No formal vow is necessary, as in the case of a *Kohen* involved in a forbidden marriage, for there the temptation to sin is much stronger than in our case. However, if a *Kohen* contaminates himself for profit, such as a doctor or pathologist who regularly handles corpses, then a formal oath of compliance with *halachah* is required before he is permitted to ascend the *duchan* (*MB* 151).

28. After the seven-day mourning period following the death of a parent, child, sibling or spouse, a *Kohen* may raise his hands, but during the seven-day mourning period he should leave the synagogue when the *Kohanim* are called (*SA* 43). The prevalent practice, however, is not to ascend the *duchan* for the full twelve-month period following the death of a parent, or the thirty-day period after one of the other relatives (*Rama* 43; *MB* 159).

Although a mourner is responsible to observe all *mitzvos* of the Torah, a mourning *Kohen* is an exception because *Bircas Kohanim* must be bestowed joyfully and good heartedly. Accordingly, during the full mourning period, a *Kohen* should leave the synagogue before the call to the *Kohanim* is issued. This applies even on the Sabbath [when a public display of mourning is forbidden] and even if he is the only *Kohen* present. If he did not leave the synagogue in time, however, or if he was asked to ascend, then he must pronounce the blessing (*MB* 157).

29. If no *Kohanim* are present at a prayer service during which *Bircas Kohanim* would ordinarily be pronounced, the prayer 'Our God, and the God of our fathers, bless us with the blessing …,' is recited by the *chazzan* before שִׂים שָׁלוֹם. In such a case the congregation should not respond *amen* after each verse, but כֵּן יְהִי רָצוֹן, *May such be His will* (*SA* 127:2).

When he recites the words יְבָרֶכְךָ ה', the *chazzan* should face the Ark; for וְיִשְׁמְרֶךָ he should turn his face to the right. Upon saying יָאֵר ה' he should face the Ark; for פָּנָיו אֵלֶיךָ וִיחֻנֶּךָּ he should turn to the left. During the final verse he should turn in neither direction but should face the Ark for the entire recitation (*MB* 127:5).